SPIRITUAL APPRENTICESHIP

Opening the Door of Promotion

by
Mark Carrillo

Unless otherwise noted, quotations are taken from the
King James Version of the Bible.

ISBN: 1-56267-205-3
Copyright ©1999 by Mark Carrillo
1701 Oakhurst Scenic Drive
Fort Worth, Texas 76111

All rights reserved

Printed in the United States of America

Table of Contents

1	MINISTER OF GOD	1
2	PAUL AND TIMOTHY	5
3	THE ANOINTING IS ACTIVATED THROUGH AUTHORITY	9
4	THE TRANSFER OF ANOINTING	17
5	SPIRITUAL APPRENTICESHIP	23
6	HISTORICAL APPRENTICESHIP	27
7	APPRENTICESHIP IS A COVENANT RELATIONSHIP	39
8	"DANCE WITH THE ONE THAT BRUNG YA" — LOYALTY	43
9	OBEDIENCE	49
10	BEING A "PASTOR'S FRIEND"	55
11	BEWARE OF EXCESSES	65
12	FAITHFULNESS IN LITTLE THINGS WILL LAUNCH YOU INTO BIG THINGS	73
13	ENCOURAGEMENT TO THOSE SEEKING PROMOTION	79
14	GETTING ON A CHURCH STAFF AND STAYING	89
15	ATTITUDES THAT BLOCK PROMOTION	93
16	TOO MUCH TOO SOON	101
17	REMINDER TO LEADERS	105
	CONCLUSION	111

FOREWORD

Mark Carrillo has worked as my associate minister at Calvary Cathedral since 1988. He is very qualified to speak on apprenticeship because he has a proven track record of being a servant, yet he has his own gifted ministry. He is a loyal team player, a man of prayer and the Word. Mark is a highly effective speaker with a strong anointing to preach, teach, disciple, and persuade others to follow Christ. So many young staff ministers are so busy with their own agenda that they miss God's agenda, the perfect will of God for their lives. Because Mark's priorities are in order, I have seen his ministry gifts continue to grow and soar. His marriage, home and finances are in divine order. Mark is a devoted husband and father.

The greatest ministry training in the world is on-the-job training, working with a seasoned, successful pastor. Many ministries are short-lived or never rise to full potential because they were thrust too quickly into the ministry without adequate preparation. Eugene H. Peterson, in the foreword to the book of Philippians in *The Message*, has said, "An apprentice acquires skill by daily and intimate association with a 'master,' picking up subtle but absolutely essential things, such as timing and rhythm and *touch*."

Because Mark Carrillo has been willing to be a team player and a servant, he is eminently qualified to write a book that is long overdue on spiritual apprenticeship. I love, trust, and respect Mark, and I strongly encourage you to read this book several times and pass it on to others.

— *Bob Nichols*
Senior Pastor,
Calvary Cathedral International
Fort Worth, Texas

ACKNOWLEDGEMENTS

I want to extend a special thank you to Pastor Bob Nichols for being a positive example of the spiritual apprenticeship principle. Many of the key points of this book are so beautifully displayed in his life.

I want to express thanks to Barbara Pendleton for her invaluable assistance, and to all those who helped with the research and writing of this book. The names are many, and God will honor the part each and every one played in writing the vision and making it plain.

I also want to thank those who have apprenticed with me. We have worked together and grown together. In many ways, you have taught me the material in this book.

PREFACE

In March of 1992, something significant happened to me that changed my life forever. I was longing for more of God and to see the strong call He placed on my life come to fruition. There was a deep yearning and a frustration within me and I had been crying out to the Lord. I knew that there *had* to be a way "to get there from here," but I wasn't sure how. While my wife and I were on vacation, the Lord began to speak to me and show me things out of his Word in direct response to those deep cries of my heart. As He spoke and laid out each point, I wrote as fast as I could to get it all down on paper. Habakkuk 2:2-3 says, *"And the Lord answered me, and said, Write the vision, and make it plain upon tables, that he may run that readeth it. For the vision is yet for an appointed time, but at the end it shall speak, and not lie: though it tarry, wait for it; because it will surely come, it will not tarry."* This book is the result of the things the Lord outlined for me that day.

MINISTER OF GOD

"...Timotheus, our brother, and minister of God..."
1 Thessalonians 3:2

For years the cry of my heart has been, "I want to be a man of God." What is the secret? I am not talking about becoming a preacher or receiving a paycheck from a ministry. I don't mean merely to step into the anointing for special assignments, but to walk in the anointing, to flow in the anointing, and to live in the anointing — even in my daily affairs. I was insatiably hungry for the presence of God. I am talking about living in His presence and letting His Spirit flow through every aspect of my life. In addition, God had planted big dreams in my heart and I was longing to see them come to pass. I have heard other people express that same longing, "God, I believe you want to bring this to pass in my life, but when? How?"

I believe God showed me the "secret" in March of 1992 while my wife and I were on vacation in a cabin on Lake Murray in Oklahoma. It was a good way to get out of the city for awhile, with no television, no radio — no distractions. It was cold that day, and there weren't many people around. I had pulled out the chaise lounge to spend some time in the Word of God and in prayer. In the course of my daily Bible reading, I came to the following Scripture:

> *"Wherefore when we could no longer forbear, we thought it good to be left at Athens alone; and sent Timotheus, our brother, and **minister of God**, and our fellowlabourer in the gospel of Christ, to establish you, and to comfort you concerning your faith."*
>
> 1 Thessalonians 3:1-2

Volumes of revelation flowed out to me, like a gusher, from that one verse. The answer to my heart's cry jumped from the page and it has been with me ever since. "Minister of God" — these words birthed something inside of me. In my heart I was saying, "Yes, God, that is the answer, but what do you mean by minister of God?" God responded, *"Well, you want to be a man of God?"* He said, *"If you want to flow in the anointing, you are going to have to get to the place of service."*

The anointing comes for a purpose: to help people.

When Paul referred to Timothy, he called him a minister of God. The word "minister" is from the Greek word *diakonos*, which simply means to run errands, to be an attendant, to serve in the menial tasks of life. Rather than putting them up on a pedestal as some people do, God sees ministers as the people serving Him in the menial tasks of life. He sees them as His attendants who run errands for Him. Timothy was a minister of God.

God then began to show me that there is a principle that flows throughout the Bible. That principle is apprenticeship. Now, I want to be clear from the beginning. Many people use the words "mentorship" and "apprenticeship" interchangeably, but this is certainly not accurate. Contrary to popular belief, the words have different meanings. Both scenarios are beneficial to the Body of Christ and help us to grow spiritually, but the difference between mentorship and apprenticeship is like the difference between being familiar with something, and actually enrolling in school to study and get a degree in the subject.

In a mentorship relationship, you have respect or admiration for a person and they may have some input or influence in your life. You may or may not have regular personal contact with them, perhaps getting together with them for lunch every so often, but there is not a binding commitment between the two parties for instruction or discipling.

In an apprenticeship relationship, the commitment is much deeper. It is an expressed agreement and commitment that truly benefits both parties involved. We will go more into this later on.

As the Lord revealed this principle to me, He began to take me through a list of men in the Word of God who served and were apprenticed by older men who were anointed of God. Joshua served Moses, Elisha served Elijah, Samuel served Eli, David served Saul. The list could go on and on. Each of these men was a minister to the man of God. They ministered to them, according to the meaning of the word in Hebrew, *as one who waits on a table*. They performed the menial tasks. They made themselves available to be directed in the day-to-day areas of life. As the Holy Spirit began to deal with me, I realized that these other men and Timothy had what I wanted: I wanted to be a minister of God.

PAUL AND TIMOTHY

After re-reading 1 Thessalonians 3:1-2, I wondered how did Timothy get to this place? The apostle Paul had confidence in him. We could say that Timothy is the New Testament poster child for apprenticeship. Timothy came from a mixed background. His mother was a Jew, but his father was a Greek (Acts 16:1). Based on what the Bible says about Timothy and his life, and the fact that he was uncircumcised as a child, some scholars believe that his father may have been a pagan (see Acts 16:3). Others believe that perhaps his father died while Timothy was quite young leaving him to be raised by his mother and grandmother. At any rate, Timothy had some things to overcome by the world's standards.

The devil would like to convince many people that they can't be used of God because of their family background. It's a good thing that Timothy didn't buy into that lie! The devil may tell us all the "reasons" why we couldn't possibly be powerful in the Kingdom of God, but we must be like Timothy and say "no" to him. James 4:7 says that we are to resist the devil and he will flee. We resist the devil by agreeing with God's Word and speaking it forth. *"I can do all things through Christ which strengtheneth me"* (Philippians 4:13); I am a new creation in Christ because 2 Corinthians 5:17 says that *"if any man be in Christ, he is a new creature: old things are passed away; behold, all things are become new."* Timothy overcame a troubled past to become a powerful figure in the Kingdom of God, and we can too!

The Bible also says that Timothy was a disciple and that he had a good reputation among the brethren (Acts 16:1-2). Paul took Timothy with him "on the road." Timothy became his companion and apprentice. Paul even referred to Timothy as his son. Timothy lived with Paul and served him. I have discovered that when we serve someone, we get really close to them. When we serve someone with our full heart, that service allows us to come into a place that few people can share. This is a place that allows us to observe and to learn from their lives. With Paul and Timothy, there was a one-on-one, committed, quality relationship in which Timothy learned from Paul, the master, and Paul poured his life into Timothy, the apprentice. Timothy was Paul's son in the ministry.

How did Timothy become the minister of God? He served the man of God. Timothy was available to minister to Paul in whatever area he needed. He went into apprenticeship with Paul, who taught him how to be alone with God just as Paul himself had been alone with God when he spent thirteen years in preparation before receiving the revelation for his ministry.

We see in further writings of Paul that as Timothy grew, he was subsequently referred to as "our brother," "minister of God," and "fellow- laborer." There was a progression. That companionship, or apprenticeship, enabled Timothy to mature in the things of God. Timothy had seen Paul deal with difficult situations. He knew how to handle things. Timothy, Paul's disciple, learned these things and came to the place where Paul could send him in his place, as a minister of God. Paul was able to say, *"Timothy is a fellow laborer. He is a man of God, and I am sending him to you in my place. He has my anointing; he has my heart. He is trustworthy and has received the anointing because he has served me well, as unto the Lord. I can, with all faith, send him to you, knowing that he will be a channel of blessing to you and take care of things just as I would."*

Timothy was sent to minister in Macedonia (Acts 19:22), in Corinth (1 Corinthians 4:17; 16:10-11 and 2 Corinthians 1:19), in Philippi (Philippians 2:19, 23), as well as Thessolonica. Timothy had moved from the position of being only a helper, to being a man of authority. He had learned the steps of fellowship with God, how to pray and how to study the Word, how to administrate and how to minister. Paul was transferring more than a title. He was transferring that heart hunger to serve God. He was imparting the mantle and anointing to wait on God and to be His servant. He was promoting Timothy into greater service.

Ultimately, Timothy was promoted to be the bishop of the church at Ephesus. Ephesus was a major area for commerce and the worship of the goddess Diana. The city was well known for demon worship, temples, shrines, and idolatrous religious images. That could be intimidating to some others, but Timothy was groomed and anointed for the position of bishop. The church at Ephesus had 3,000 members at the time, and some Bible scholars believe that Timothy was only seventeen years old when he took over the pastorate! He gave his life to be a minister of God even to the point of death, just as Paul did. Timothy learned how to be a man of God by serving the well-seasoned man of God.

THE ANOINTING IS ACTIVATED THROUGH AUTHORITY

As I looked at the life of Timothy, I saw how he served Paul and therefore he was the beneficiary of Paul's anointing. I have already referred to the anointing, and throughout this book I will mention the anointing quite frequently. But what exactly is the anointing? The term is a broad and extensive subject that has been the topic of many other books. Some have said it is the power of God, the manifest presence and power of God or even the touch of God. Others have said, it is the supernatural equipment to get the job done. The anointing is also referred to as a "rubbing off," "refreshing," "sanctification and separation" or "consecration." Those all describe the anointing correctly, but within the context of this book, let's describe the anointing as the manifested presence of God showing up to empower a person to do whatever is needed to carry out the plan of God. This includes the immediate plan of God as well as His long-term plan. This could result in the operation of various gifts of the Spirit including prophetic words, healing, miracles, etc. Let's face it — when God shows up, stuff happens.

There are a couple of things about the anointing that we need to keep in mind. First of all, the anointing is tangible. The word "tangible" means capable of being touched; and, capable of touching you. You can wait until the anointing touches you, or you can touch the anointing! Secondly, the anointing is transferable. That means it is capable of moving from one person to another. It can also be absorbed and held by material substances. Look at the following two verses.

> *"And God wrought special miracles by the hands of Paul:* **So that from his body were brought unto the sick handkerchiefs or aprons**, *and the diseases departed from them, and the evil spirits went out of them."*
> Acts 19:11-12

> *And Elisha died, and they buried him. And the bands of the Moabites invaded the land at the coming in of the year. And it came to pass, as they were burying a man, that, behold, they spied a band of men; and they cast the man into the sepulchre of Elisha: and when the man was let down, and* **touched the bones of Elisha**, *he revived, and stood up on his feet."*
> 2 Kings 13:20-21

It wasn't the handkerchiefs or Elisha's bones that did miracles when they were used or touched, it was the anointing that was permeating them that healed, delivered and resurrected the dead!

The Anointing Is Activated Through Authority

We can read about the woman with the issue of blood who touched Jesus' anointing. When she *touched the hem of His garment* she was healed:

> *"... When she had heard of Jesus, came in the press behind, and **touched his garment**. For she said, If I may touch but his clothes, I shall be whole. And straightway the fountain of her blood was dried up; and she felt in her body that she was healed of that plague. And Jesus, immediately knowing in himself that **virtue had gone out of him**, turned him about in the press, and said, **Who touched my clothes?"***
>
> Mark 5:27-30

She didn't wait for hands to be laid on her, she laid hands on Him! SHE TOUCHED THE ANOINTING! We do not have to idly sit and wait for God to touch us. The things of God are not going to drop into our laps like ripe cherries off of a tree. Just as we are to pursue things in the natural, even more so we are to pursue God. Not just His gifts or blessings, but HIM. Everything we need is found in the presence of God. We just need to push through any and every obstacle that would stand in our way, to get there.

There is only one anointing and it is God's. I am thankful that He has not left us to ourselves to try to figure things out on our own. He has ordained a way for us to fulfill the call He has placed on our lives. Whether we are called into ministry, missions, business, teaching, or parenting, God has deposited an anointing within us specifically for the task. Our dreams or vision may seem impossible, but we are not as far from the door of promotion as we may think. Jesus walked in His anointing to pray, to bring healing to the multitudes, to feed the hungry, and to deliver those captured by sin. It is God's will that we walk in that anointing, too.

Many people talk a lot about anointing — receiving it and flowing in it — but for our anointing to grow and increase, it must operate under authority. Someone may have a tremendous anointing, but if it is not working under authority, it is not going to produce all that God has designed for it to produce. It becomes unfulfilled potential. Sadly enough, unfulfilled potential is a common problem today.

God is looking for carriers — people on whom He can pour out the anointing who will touch others for Him. He is looking for people with no agenda other than that of the Holy Spirit. He's seeking people who are willing to lose their lives for the sake of the Gospel. We must understand that it is important to activate the flow of anointing so that we are giving as well as receiving, which means there will be a fresh flow of God's power through us all the time. Here is the principle that the Holy Spirit shared with me: *The anointing is activated through authority.* This means that the anointing will be activated through submission to lines of spiritual authority.

The Anointing Is Activated Through Authority

*"Let every soul be subject unto the higher powers. **For there is no power but of God: the powers that be are ordained of God.** Whosoever therefore resisteth the power, resisteth the ordinance of God: and they that resist shall receive to themselves damnation."*

Romans 13:1-2

Whether we think a person should be in a position of authority or not is irrelevant. The Bible clearly states that God is the one who allows people to be in authority. If a person will not submit to the ones that God has set up as their authority here on earth, that person cannot properly submit to God either. Without exception.

No attempt to usurp authority will ever be blessed.

One of the gravest examples of usurping authority is shown in Judas Iscariot's betrayal of Jesus. When Jesus was delivered to Pilate for judgment, Pilate asked Jesus, "Don't you realize that I have the power to crucify you, or I have the power to release you?" Here is where Jesus made the point very clear. Pilate was operating in his God-given role of authority. However, Judas decided to overthrow the proper chain of command. He tried to put himself in a position above Jesus by turning Him over for selfish gain.

*"Jesus answered, Thou couldest have no power at all against me, except it were given thee from above: **therefore he that delivered me unto thee hath the greater sin.**"*

John 19:11

Usurping authority is rebellion and it does not always have to manifest itself through out-and-out insubordination. Rebellion is a wrong heart attitude which grows when fed with negative thoughts like "I don't like them," "Who do they think they are?" or "I can do a better job than they can." It gains more strength when it starts coming out of a person's mouth with negative comments. Proverbs 18:4 says, *"The words of a man's mouth are as deep waters..."* Our mouths are fountains and our words are the water that comes out of that fountain.

> *"Out of the same mouth proceedeth blessing and cursing. My brethren, these things ought not so to be. Doth a fountain send forth at the same place sweet water and bitter?"*
>
> James 3:10-11

In reality, a person who murmurs and complains among their peers about the pastor or his staff is spewing out bitter water, which is offensive to God. We must only allow sweet water — positive words of life and blessing — to come out. We cannot expect God's anointing to flow freely in our lives if we are spewing bitter water.

In 1 Samuel 24 we can read about when Saul was trying to kill David. David fled and hid in the caves of Engedi. David's men were all ready to capture Saul and to deliver him to David. David was able to sneak in and cut off a piece of Saul's robe. He could have felt good about himself because he didn't kill Saul when he had the opportunity. But, instead, David fell under great conviction.

The Anointing Is Activated Through Authority

> "... David's heart smote him, because he had cut off Saul's skirt. And he said unto his men, The LORD forbid that I should do this thing unto my master, the LORD's anointed, to stretch forth mine hand against him, seeing he is the anointed of the LORD. So David stayed his servants with these words, and suffered them not to rise against Saul."
>
> 1 Samuel 24:5-7

David had a clear understanding of God-given authority. He knew that God was the one who anointed and set Saul in his place of authority. Any attack against this authority would be an attack against the authority of God.

Watch and learn

> "Then answered Jesus and said unto them, Verily, verily, I say unto you, The Son can do nothing of himself, but what he seeth the Father do: for what things soever he doeth, these also doeth the Son likewise."
>
> John 5:19

> "I can of mine own self do nothing: as I hear, I judge: and my judgment is just; because I seek not mine own will, but the will of the Father which hath sent me."
>
> John 5:30

Jesus was anointed without measure, yet He would do nothing He did not see the Father do first. When He was a boy, he submitted himself to the authority of his parents (Luke 2:51). His anointing was activated through submission to authority. Jesus, when He came in the flesh, put Himself in the place of an apprentice, a servant. He watched what the Master did, and He was obedient to what He saw.

> *"Who, being in the form of God, thought it not robbery to be equal with God:* **But made himself of no reputation, and took upon him the form of a servant,** *and was made in the likeness of men: And being found in fashion as a man, he humbled himself, and became obedient unto death, even the death of the cross. Wherefore God also hath highly exalted him, and given him a name which is above every name."*
>
> Philippians 2:6-9

Jesus watched the Father and did what He saw Him do. Then, it became His task to turn around and train His disciples. This is apprenticeship in action. Once the Twelve had seen Him and studied what He did, they were then commissioned to go and do likewise. Before anyone can be a leader, they must become a servant. If someone cannot submit, they cannot lead. The transfer of the anointing will always follow surrender and submission in the life of the person who is called to serve.

God wants to do mighty demonstrations of the Spirit that can happen only when we begin to flow with the Holy Spirit's authority. It is time for us to stop being spectators and to step into the anointing, which is not only for demonstration in the church, but also for our daily lives. This anointing works in the marketplace, in relationships, and in demonstrations of signs, wonders, and miracles. God wants it to operate through you and me. But we must remember that the anointing is activated through authority.

THE TRANSFER OF ANOINTING

"And he [Jesus] goeth up into a mountain, and calleth unto him whom he would: and they came unto him. And he ordained twelve, that they should be with him, and that he might send them forth to preach, and to have power to heal sicknesses, and to cast out devils."

Mark 3:13-15

Just as Jesus called the Twelve to commune with Him, He has also called us to commune with Him — to stay in His presence — because He wants to transfer the power to heal sicknesses, to cast out devils and to perform other things at His command. But there is a process to the transfer of the anointing. God will set us up with divine connections and divine appointments to form relationships with key people, but before these relationships are formed, our relationship with the Lord should be well-established. The anointing is transferred through association, contact and service. I will go into these in more detail in later chapters, but I want to briefly touch on it here.

First of all we must be in right relationship with the Father. As born again believers in Jesus Christ, God is now our Father. Some people, however, have a wrong view of the Father, thinking of Him as a mean old man with a bat, waiting to smack us whenever we mess up. But when we understand the love the Father has for us, we will be bold in moving out in the things of the Spirit without the fear of making mistakes. He lovingly corrects us, but He never rejects us. There is an atmosphere of total love and acceptance in the Father's presence. Just like any parent gets excited when their child takes their first steps, He will applaud every attempt we make to flow with Him. Can you imagine a parent hollering at their child or spanking them for falling down when they're learning how to walk? That would be abusive! Instead, they lovingly help the child get back up and encourage them to try again, cheering them on the whole way. When we have received the Spirit of adoption (Galatians 4:4-6), we can boldly step out to obey the Spirit's promptings and to move in a stronger anointing, because we know that the Father is only going to cheer us on. Then, God will send people into our lives to nurture and encourage us. They, too, will cheer us on and lovingly correct us so that we become more mature and stable in the things of God.

Association

"The disciple is not above his master: but every one that is perfect shall be as his master."

Luke 6:40

"Verily, verily, I say unto you, He that believeth on me, the works that I do shall he do also; and greater works than these shall he do; because I go unto my Father."
John 14:12

"And he ordained twelve, that they should be with him, and that he might send them forth to preach."
Mark 3:14

Maturity comes through believing the Word and being in the presence of God. By spending time with Him we will know the Master. Then we will be like Him and be able to do the works that He does. We can gain insight and receive a transfer of the anointing by carefully listening to the admonitions of the key people with whom God joins us — association. We begin to be partakers of that anointing by having a receptive attitude. When we see the anointing flowing through them, we can say, "Yes, that's it. I receive that for my life." Every time they open their mouth, we can learn something. By heeding their teaching and gleaning from the things we see in their ministry, we can receive that same anointing and flow in it ourselves. The same anointing that operates in their lives will begin to operate in our lives by association.

Contact

The Bible is clear that another way the anointing is transferred is through contact by the laying on of hands. It was obviously wrong to try to buy the gifts of God, but Simon the sorcerer recognized the power of the anointing and how the apostles transferred it. He wanted that power so much that he wanted to buy it.

> *"Then laid they their hands on them, and they received the Holy Ghost. And when Simon saw that through laying on of the apostles' hands the Holy Ghost was given, he offered them money."*
>
> Acts 8:17-18

What Simon failed to understand was that the Holy Spirit is the source of the power and He cannot be bought. God has always been more concerned about the heart than the gift, or the ministry of men. He has shown us that He expects us to guard the anointing and to use caution in the distribution of it. Using contact as a means for imparting the anointing is a serious matter to God, and it should be handled with respect and godly wisdom.

> *"Lay hands suddenly on no man, neither be partaker of other men's sins: keep thyself pure."*
>
> 1 Timothy 5:22

Hands were laid on King Saul. He was anointed, but we read in 1 Samuel 15 and 16 that he strayed away from God, so the Lord rejected him. It is a sad picture of what can happen to a heart that does not stay humble and yielded before God. God needed a replacement — a man after His own heart. Jesse had a son, little David. He wasn't passing out business cards, he was working in the field. He was minding his business, serving and taking care of the sheep. He was doing the menial tasks. God instructed Samuel to lay hands on David to transfer the anointing and to commission him for service (1 Sam. 16:12-13). David was faithful in doing the manual labor that was set before him. That set him up to receive the transfer of the anointing and ultimately promotion, but he wasn't promoted immediately. Many people think that David succeeded Saul as King of Israel, but it was Ishbosheth, Saul's son, who was appointed king (see 2 Samuel 2). David had to wait for God's appointed time of promotion, with a good attitude.

Service

Much more than by merely associating with someone, or coming in contact with them, the anointing is transferred by *serving* an anointed minister of God. Joshua served Moses. Elisha served Elijah. The disciples served Jesus. I will go much more in depth on this subject later on, but the most intensive way for the anointing to be transferred is through service.

The greater the service, the greater the transfer of anointing.

The transfer of the anointing can clearly be seen in various degrees by looking at many of the well-known ministries of today. Kathryn Kuhlman had one of the most tremendous anointings of her era. She was greatly influenced by another powerful woman of God named Aimee Semple McPherson, and even attended McPherson's Bible School in California. Worldwide healing minister, Benny

Hinn, was greatly influenced by Kuhlman's ministry. Do you see the progression? Aimee Semple McPherson — Kathryn Kuhlman — Benny Hinn. Whether it be through association, contact, or service, the ministry of each one of the following people greatly affected the heart of the next.

- John Alexander Dowie, 1847-1907
- Charles Parham, 1873-1929
- Maria Woodworth-Etter, 1844-1924
- Aimee Semple McPherson, 1890-1944
- Kathryn Kuhlman, 1907-1976
- Benny Hinn, 1952 - **

While there are, of course, other spiritual genealogies and other lineages with anointings that are just as powerful, the above illustrates my point. We can benefit from the anointing and learn from the mistakes of those who have gone before us. Association, contact, and service opens the channel for the blessing and anointing to be transferred to anyone who is willing to get in position to receive.

SPIRITUAL APPRENTICESHIP

Even more powerful than just being familiar with a ministry and being influenced by their teaching is when a person gets linked up in an apprenticeship relationship with a father or mother of faith. This is where the real power in association comes in. I like to say it this way, "If you want big fleas, hang out with the big dogs." It is God's will that we grow from faith to faith, that we increase from strength to strength, from glory to glory, from victory to victory, all of which comes through association. No relationship — no transfer; it goes hand in hand. Apprenticeship dramatically accelerates the growth process. Spiritual apprenticeship is how the anointing is transferred from generation to generation. A spiritual apprentice is one bound by a covenant agreement to serve a man of God for the purpose of training, instruction in the Word, and transfer of the anointing.

We have an anointing, but God wants to take us to a higher level of intensity. We get this intensity in the prayer closet with God and from watching other people's ministries, but I thank God that He also gives us hands-on people to disciple and apprentice us. Some things are not taught, they must be caught. We catch the spirit of those with whom we spend time. We catch their spark of faith.

> *"A man's gift maketh room for him, and bringeth him before great men."*
> Proverbs 18:16

If we are faithful to God in the little things, our gifts will make room for us. We will come into relationships with men and women of God who are at a higher level in the things of God than we are. God will set us up with people who dream big and think big. People who are ready to "go for it" for God and who are willing to pour that same Spirit into us. God wants us to make divine connections with men and women of God so that we can glean from their lives and experience. They have wisdom that is from above, and they want to sow into the lives of others. The point is,

God wants you to fulfill your call, and He will use people to help train you to do that.

In a God-ordained spiritual apprenticeship, you will reap blessings and benefits that others will not have simply because they are not willing to pay the price. They do not understand that the pieces don't fit, until you commit. Apprenticeship requires commitment. Apprenticeship requires some personal sacrifice.

As we've already seen, the anointing is transferred through association, service and contact. Jesus called twelve men not to *work for* Him, but to *be with* Him so that He could spend time with them. He wanted to apprentice them; to impart into their lives both the principles and the application of the anointing. Another good example of a spiritual apprentice is Elisha. In 2 Kings 3, when the king of Moab rebelled against King Jehoram of Israel, Jehoram sought advice from King Jehoshaphat of Judah. Jehoshaphat immediately asked for a prophet of God.

> "... **Here is Elisha the son of Shaphat, which poured water on the hands of Elijah.**"
> 2 Kings 3:11

Elisha poured water over the hands of the prophet. That meant that Elisha helped the prophet wash his hands. Elisha performed the menial tasks for Elijah. This is the type of man who did the laundry, cut the lawn, set up the tape table, and vacuumed the carpet. He was not in the public eye, but in the background. Some people have the idea that ministry is only preaching, but I encourage you to take on the role of a true minister of God. Choose to be someone who serves and who runs errands. Again, *the greater the service, the greater the transfer of the anointing*. If you want a greater anointing, find a place to serve faithfully in the your local church body.

Sometimes we see people whose anointings are not operating even though they seem to have received hundreds of prophecies. They have a new suit of clothes and a new Bible, but not enough power to swat a fly. That is when we should look at their service life. Who are they serving? Who are they attached to? If people knew how service affects the level of the anointing in their lives, *they would fight for the right to serve*. They would fight for the right to sing in the choir or minister to children. They would say, "Get out of my way. I'm going to be an usher." Why? **Because service brings the anointing in a greater way than any other activity.**

Elisha was called to be a prophet of God, yet he became an apprentice, a servant. He willingly became the one who washed the dishes, did the laundry, and took care of everything Elijah needed. He understood the value of apprenticeship.

If you want to receive the full transfer of the anointing, find a man or woman of God to serve. Pray for God to set it all up for you, and then keep your eyes and ears open. When God makes that connection, serve with all of your heart. Then the anointing will not only be added to your life, it will be multiplied exponentially. Between the coming of the anointing and the call being activated in our lives, there is a period of service, testing and proving — a time of apprenticeship.

HISTORICAL APPRENTICESHIP

Every spiritual principle has an example in the natural. When we talk about serving the man or woman of God, we are talking about a spiritual apprenticeship. When God showed me this principle, He launched me into a study on apprenticeship. I became interested in knowing the answer to the question, "What is an apprentice and what does it have to do with being a minister of God?" In my quest I found some very interesting parallels between being a servant of God and apprenticeship as it was reflected throughout history. Stick with me. This is good stuff. If we look at this information under the guidance of the Holy Spirit, we can clearly see that apprenticeship runs everywhere through the Bible and it is something pertinent to our lives as believers.

The dictionary definition of an apprentice is: *one who is bound by a legal agreement to work for another person in exchange for education or instruction in a trade, art, or business.* Maybe you remember from your history classes that the apprentice would go to live with his master. He would eat with him, work with him, and train with him until, at some point, he would emerge with the skill to do the master's trade. Most people have probably not thought about apprenticeship since their history classes, or, if they have, their response is something like, "Apprenticeship — that was something that happened in Paul Revere's day."

Actually, the first records of apprenticeship I found go back to the Twenty-first Century B.C. An early king of Babylon, named Hammurabi, implemented laws that basically demanded that all artisans and craftsmen teach their trades to young people. I was excited to find this out because *this ties directly in with Biblical history.* In 606 B.C., Daniel was exiled to Babylon. Although he was a slave, for all practical purposes he was treated as an apprentice and adopted into the king's court. The court became responsible for his livelihood, his education, and his well being. When he had fulfilled his apprenticeship, he became one of the leaders of the kingdom even though he was still an exile in captivity.

In the Fifth Century B.C. Greek culture, contracts showed that craftsmen who had apprentices could charge a higher rate. They recognized the definite benefits of transferring their knowledge through the generations.

The ancient Jewish culture also put a high priority on the training of youth. Remember that they didn't have teaching tapes and videos. They made certain that the Torah —

the Law — was passed down so that their culture and traditions would not be forgotten.

In ancient Rome, most of the craftsmen originally were slaves. During this time a standard- bearing organization was set up and called collegia, from which we draw our word *"college."* The collegia set and maintained the standards of excellence and trade.

In Egypt, young men were taken from their families and sent to skilled craftsmen as apprentices to learn a trade. Again we see this in the Bible. Joseph's brothers sold him into slavery and he wound up in Egypt (Genesis 37:28). But he was not treated as a slave for long. Instead, he was taken into Potiphar's house, where after a period of apprenticeship, he took care of Potiphar's household and financial affairs (Genesis 39:4). Even after being sent to prison, Joseph was well equipped to run things. He had been trained to the point that he was put in charge of the prison (Genesis 39:21-23). The favor of God was continually upon Joseph. He flowed in his anointing and waited on the Lord. Joseph was at last brought before Pharaoh to interpret some disturbing dreams. Pharaoh recognized the wisdom God had bestowed upon Joseph. He knew Joseph was well equipped to take care of his kingdom. Pharaoh said,

> *"Thou shalt be over my house, and according unto thy word shall all my people be ruled: only in the throne will I be greater than thou."*
>
> Genesis 41:40

Spiritual Apprenticeship

By the Twelfth and Thirteenth Centuries in England, apprenticeship had developed into a common practice. The apprenticeship, confirmed by a legal contract, took place while the apprentice was between the ages of fourteen and twenty-one.

During the 1600's in colonial New England, when a family could not financially support all of their children, they would take one of the children who was under ten years old, and contract them out — or *indenture* them — into a binding apprenticeship relationship. Several copies of the contract were made, and all of the parties involved signed each copy. All of the copies of the signed contracts were stacked together and then a small tear was made through the stack. That way if there was ever a question of whether a contract was a true copy of the original agreement or not, they could line up the copy in question with the other copies of the contract. If the tear — or the *indenture* —lined up correctly, they knew the contract was valid. That's why contracts were called *indentures*. Indentures consisted of three major parts:

- The requirements of the apprentice
- The provisions the master would make, and
- The reward at the end of the apprenticeship

The following is an excerpt from such an indenture made in 1676. This indenture was signed by his parents, covering the apprenticeship of a boy named Nathan Knight.

Historical Apprenticeship

This Indenture witnesseth that I, Nathan Knight have put myself apprentice to Samuel Whidden, of Portsmouth, in the county of Portsmouth, mason, and bound after the manner of an apprentice with him to serve and abide the full space and term of twelve years and five months during which time the said apprentice his said master faithfully shall serve. He shall not contract matrimony within the said time. The goods of his said master, he shall not spend or lend. He shall not play cards, or dice, or any other unlawful game, whereby his said master may have damage in his own goods, or others. Taverns, he shall not haunt, nor from his master's business absent himself by day or by night, but in all things shall behave himself as a faithful apprentice ought to do. And the said master his said apprentice shall teach and instruct, or cause to be taught and instructed in the art and mystery as mason; finding unto his said apprentice during the said time meat, drink, washing, lodging, and apparel, fitting an apprentice, teaching him to read, and allowing him three months towards the latter end of his time to go to school to write, and also double apparel at end of said time.

Think of it. If this young man served until he was twenty-one, that means this contract was made when he was only eight and a half years old!

Spiritual Apprenticeship

In 1747, London-born artist William Hogarth did a series of twelve artistic prints named *Industry and Idleness* based on George Lillo's 1731 domestic tragedy *The London Merchant.* In this series, Hogarth chronicles the lives of two men beginning from the time they were young apprentices in the weaving industry. In the first print, both men are depicted at weaving looms while they were in apprenticeship. One apprentice, whose frame is inscribed *Industry*, is working diligently. The other frame shows that the other apprentice, inscribed as *Idleness*, is asleep on the job as the master is coming in with a big stick to wake him up. Under *Industry* is a quotation from Proverbs 10:4, *"The hand of the diligent maketh rich,"* but under *Idleness* is written, *"The drunkard...shall come to poverty; and drowsiness shall clothe a man with rags"* (Proverbs 23:21). The next prints in the series show the paths the men take throughout life. They depict success and happiness for *Industry,* and sordid living and misery for *Idleness.* The series ends with the idle apprentice being hanged and the industrious one becoming the lord mayor of London. To them, apprenticeship was serious business and your character as an apprentice would determine the outcome of your life.

Under the system of apprenticeship of that day, the apprentice was adopted by the family with whom he was apprenticed. The family would not only be responsible for teaching the young man the trade, but they were also responsible to give him a good education, and to train him in manners and etiquette. The apprentice would earn no wages during the actual apprenticeship, but at the end of his scheduled term, the master certified that the apprentice was skilled and provided him with some tools of the trade. He gave him everything he needed to get started on his own.

Remember that word, *collegia*? Our *colleges* today use methods for apprenticeship training that are very similar to those used back then. Even the language is the same language that was used in Bible times. Have you ever heard of a Master's Degree or a Master Technician? Historical apprenticeship is the background for those terms. Being a *master* meant being one who was highly skilled in a trade and who was qualified to teach it to others. The master was a skilled craftsman who had fully met all of the guild standards of excellence. He had all the tools and knew what to do. He knew how to perform state-of-the-art functions and had acquired all the available knowledge for his trade. The person working with the master was the *apprentice*. The apprentice was bound to the master for a specified period of time to be trained, tested and evaluated. A *journeyman* was someone who had moved beyond that place of apprenticeship. He was no longer in that daily one-on-one training relationship, but he was able to go out and work for a daily wage to accumulate enough capital and experience to completely launch out on his own. Then, he would build something — on his own — that would demonstrate the skills he had acquired from the master. That's where the term *masterpiece* comes from. He did the works his master had shown him. He became perfected. He moved from being a student, who was faithful where he was called, into being a craftsman, fully functioning within his calling. The masterpiece showed that he himself was now a master.

Many famous Americans began their work as apprentices. Among them were Paul Revere and Benjamin Franklin. The practice of apprenticeship still continues today. In fact, at the time of this writing, according to the Bureau of Apprenticeship and Training, in the United States an estimated 37,000 sponsors offer registered apprenticeship training to approximately 431,800 apprentices annually.

An apprenticeship always looked toward the apprentice's future, as well as to preserve a heritage. Spiritual apprenticeship establishes our future in a covenant relationship. Apprenticeship historically has to do with natural things. Remember that Jesus apprenticed under Joseph, His earthly father, and learned to be a carpenter. But there is *spiritual* apprenticeship as well. Jesus was also under spiritual tutoring. He learned about the Law and the Prophets from the standard training that was provided to young Hebrew boys at the local synagogue. By the age of twelve or thirteen He astonished the Pharisees and teachers in the temple in Jerusalem with His under-

Historical Apprenticeship

standing of the Law by His questions. The Bible says He learned and grew in knowledge. He learned through obedience to His earthly parents, by what He was taught and through prayer and fellowship with the Heavenly Father.

If we transfer this concept to our own spiritual walk, we see that Jesus desires to train us in the things to which we are called. He has given us gifts and the tools. Now He is going to train us by His relationship with us and by the relationship He has with other men and women. This is what will bring us into the place of full-time service, step by step.

I have a personal respect for apprenticeship because prior to entering the ministry, I wanted to learn a trade. Even the apostle Paul had a trade as a tentmaker (Acts 18:1-3). I wanted to have a skill I could always do if I needed to. Right up until the time he went on to be with the Lord, my stepfather did stone masonry work; laying brick, rock and blocks. So when I was younger, I worked with him, shoveling sand, mixing mortar, carrying rocks, and doing lots of hard work in all kinds of weather — including the scorching Texas summers. I remember that at times I thought, "God, I would sure like to go to heaven right now because I know it would be cooler there." I spent most of the time shoveling sand and emptying big cement sacks into a huge, noisy mixer. Each sack has little pores in it so that when it hits something, the pressure is relieved and it won't break open. The impact causes dust to fly out through the pores. I lifted tons of those sacks of cement and threw them on top of the mixer. Then I would break open the sack and dust would billow all around me. It was just plain hard, gritty, dirty work. I did this all through college, working part-time after classes. After graduation I decided to stick with it. In that particular industry, it takes about three years to learn everything that needs to be done and to actually practice those skills. I wanted to know how to do it *right*.

You learn by association. You do not start out being what the master is or doing what he does, but your target is to eventually be like the master. The day will come when the master lets you use the trowel a little bit, or if you are a carpenter, the saw. You start out at the bottom, learning the basics. The stone mason never mixes any of the mud himself. His workers or apprentices do that. But, he mixed up *thousands* of batches before he was qualified to be a mason. To become a good stone mason, first you must develop knowledge of sand, grit, and water. Then you move on from there.

It is at the point of hard work that many people get washed out of the spiritual apprenticeship program. They do not remain faithful to the master in the small things. They do not see how shoveling sand and taking mud to a master (who is already doing what the apprentice wants to be doing) has anything to do with their calling.

Historical Apprenticeship

It is faithfulness in the day-to-day things that will be the launching pad for your own ministry.

If you cannot be a self-starter and give a man an honest day's work for your wages, if you are unwilling to give more effort than you are being paid for, then you are not being faithful in training — in your apprenticeship. If you cannot be faithful and serve Jesus in a secular job, please do not attempt to get into the ministry. The Scriptures tell us that Jesus trained most of His life for three years of ministry. Because He was tempted in all points as we are (Hebrews 4:15), He probably was tempted to quit, saying, "This isn't worth it. If I have to do one more carpentry job, then forget it. I'm going home." But He didn't.

Every job we do is preparation for our ministry, wherever it is and in whatever arena. By being in relationship with the Master, we not only become like Him in doing the things He does, *but we also become like Him in personality and character*. It is important to be faithful during the days when it seems as though God has given you only busywork. It is particularly important to be faithful, as Jesus was, in prayer, in the study of God's Word, and in attendance in the house of God. Carefully listening to your pastor in the pulpit is preparation. You will draw from his anointing and gift. Again, if you are not faithful in that which is another man's, Jesus asked, who will entrust you with your own? (Luke 16:12). If you want to receive the anointing, be faithful and diligent so that you will be in position to receive.

APPRENTICESHIP IS A COVENANT RELATIONSHIP

An apprenticeship relationship is a serious commitment. A spiritual apprentice is someone who is bound by covenant relationship to serve a man or woman of God to be trained, instructed in the Word, and for the transfer of anointing. When we covenant to serve a man or woman of God, we receive the advantage of his or her knowledge and experience. The revelation God has given that individual over time becomes our starting point. We can gain the benefit of what has taken them years to learn without having to go through some of the hard lessons ourselves. Talk about advantage! We must also remember that a covenant relationship is not something to be taken lightly. Look at the following excerpt from Ezekiel 17:14-15:

> *"...by keeping of his covenant it* [the kingdom] *might stand. But he rebelled... **shall he break the covenant, and be delivered?**"*

In the above passage it shows the importance of covenant. By keeping the covenant, the kingdom would stand. Breaking the covenant meant certain death. The covenant was a serious agreement that joined two parties together. The covenant bound them to fulfill certain conditions, and in exchange they received certain advantages. When a covenant was established, God was solemnly invoked as a witness, an oath was sworn, and a sign was given. The penalty for breaking a covenant was death. That really gives meaning to the Scripture James 5:12, *"...but let your yea be yea; and your nay, nay; lest ye fall into condemnation."* Apprenticeship is a covenant relationship. I can recount many stories of pastors or other men of God who had people promise that they would stick with them through thick and thin, only to find that when a challenge came their way, these same people were gone.

As we saw earlier, Elisha was in spiritual apprenticeship with Elijah. It is recorded in 1 Kings 19:19-21, that at Elijah's first call, Elisha slew his oxen — literally sacrificed his secular occupation — and ran after the man of God. Later, in 2 Kings 2, when Elijah told Elisha, "You stay here," Elisha responded, "As the Lord lives, I *will not* leave you. I will be with you until the end." Before Elisha, Elijah had a different servant. That servant was there when Elijah had the showdown with the prophets of Baal (1 Kings 18). He was there for the victory against the false prophets. He was there when the drought was broken and the rain came. Then, Jezebel sent word that she was out for blood. She was going to kill Elijah for the deaths of the false prophets.

Apprenticeship Is A Covenant Relationship

> *"And when he [Elijah] saw that, he arose, and went for his life, and came to Beersheba, which belongeth to Judah, and **left his servant there.**"*
>
> 1 Kings 19:3

I believe that Elijah presented the same option to the other servant that he later presented to Elisha saying, "You stay here." The other servant agreed to back away from Elijah during that tough time, and *we never hear about that servant again*. Elisha, however, was covenant-committed to Elijah. A covenant relationship is for the long haul, not just until the heat comes or until someone asks you to do something that you feel is beneath you.

Some people think, *"I've got an anointing. I've got a call of God on my life. Why does the pastor want me to go pick up that person and drive them around? Doesn't he see that I'm a man of God in my own right?"* If we are true ministers of God, then we will be servants doing the menial tasks with no regard for our personal reputation. Helen Keller once said, "I long to accomplish a great and noble task, but it is my chief duty to accomplish small tasks as if they were great and noble." Each of us is called to serve in the Body of Christ, whether it is by teaching a class, driving a van, or sweeping a floor. When we understand the benefit of the covenant relationship God is trying to give us, we will never again despise any task given to us.

The church is the hub of the New Testament wheel called revival and we are the spokes. If our spoke is out of place, we will find ourselves lying beside the road with revival moving on while others fill our place. But, as we take our places, wherever that may be, this wheel will roll smoothly.

8

"DANCE WITH THE ONE THAT BRUNG YA" LOYALTY

"For though ye have ten thousand instructors in Christ, yet have ye not many fathers: for in Christ Jesus I have begotten you through the gospel."

1 Corinthians 4:15

We cannot sow into a spiritual apprenticeship and not be blessed because it is God's method of carrying on His legacy in the earth. Spiritual apprenticeship is a love relationship that sometimes requires a sacrifice of our own personal agendas. There's an old saying, "Dance with the one that brung ya." In that simple phrase lies a great truth, which is loyalty. Problems sometimes surface when the anointing begins to grow on an apprentice and people start making little comments, like, "You won't be with us very long," or, "You're going to be pastoring on your own before long." Or, well-meaning people will sometimes ask a young minister, "When are you going to get your own church?" as if that would indicate that they have arrived or become a "real minister." Why is it that some people hold the local church in such low esteem that if a staff member develops an anointing, they can no longer be a part of the team? It seems that if someone has their own ministry, we esteem them, but if they serve on someone else's staff then they're not a "real" man or woman of God. In our society it seems almost blasphemous to be anything but the top person. If having one of the precious few top positions were the only hope of being fully matured, what a bleak outlook that would be for the vast majority of people. When I am confronted with the "you-won't-be-here-much-longer" mentality I think, *"Get out of my face, devil! Nothing or nobody is moving me out of my place of anointing and service!"*

The strength of our anointing increases by doing what God has called us to do. We are all serving Jesus — whether in business, as a housewife, or in full-time ministry. God is the One who assigns to us where we are to serve. And, He can reassign us at any time. We need to be sure that wherever we are right now, we serve there as though we will not be reassigned until Jesus comes back. There must always be a balance in our walk with God. Certainly there is a proper time to leave and launch out on our own, but God's best is to be "sent out" with the leadership's blessing. No bridges are burned. It is very sad to see a pastor invest time, prayer and energy into the growth of someone; only to see that person skip right out on the pastor with no sense of loyalty whatsoever. We must stay sensitive to the prompting of the Holy Ghost. We must discern the season in which He has us. We must also discern when that season changes.

One of the most dangerous times for a plant is when it is uprooted and then replanted. My wife and I had some landscaping done in our yard. We planted some beautiful flowering plants just outside the house. They were so beautiful and healthy that we wanted to bring some of the beauty into our home. So, my wife got a big attractive pot, dug up one of the plants, replanted it and brought it into the house. After a short time, we noticed that the plant didn't look very good. It didn't bloom. It was withered. The leaves all dried up and fell off. Ultimately we moved it back outside in a sad attempt to revive it. For a little while it looked like it showed signs of life, but then a freeze came. Had it not been in such a fragile state from being uprooted, it might have made it; however, the transplanting weakened its resistance and led to its demise. This can happen when believers do not remain loyal to where God has planted them.

We should never allow our own personal vision to keep us from serving somebody else's vision. In any group of people there will be different anointings, different gifts and different calls. But corporately, even though it may be multi-faceted, there is only one vision. We need to be faithful to the vision of the leader of the house. If I have a vision and my pastor has a vision, and everyone else has their own little vision, we have blurred or multiple visions.

Spiritual Apprenticeship

That can lead to **di**vision. *Division* cuts off the flow of the anointing. It is the willingness to serve that sets an apprentice apart to become a full-blown man or woman of God.

If you are unwilling to help the man of God fulfill his destiny, you will be disqualified from fulfilling your own.

At one time the Bible refers to Joshua simply as one of Moses' young men (Numbers 11:28). He was just part of the pack, just one of the boys. He was *ministering* to the needs of Moses. Later the Bible says that Joshua, *Moses' minister*, distinguished himself from among the people that were serving Moses (Numbers 27:18-23). Joshua dedicated himself to serving Moses. He was loyal.

> *"And the LORD said unto Moses, Come up to me into the mount, and be there: and I will give thee tables of stone, and a law, and commandments which I have written; that thou mayest teach them. And Moses rose up, and his minister Joshua: and Moses went up into the mount of God."*
>
> Exodus 24:12-13

In this reference, Moses was about to receive the stone tablets with the Ten Commandments. God told Moses *"Come up to me in the mount, and* ***be there****."* This is why loyalty is so important. We need to be there to draw from the gift that God has imparted to our leadership, whether things are going good or bad, whether we like the sermon or not. We need to be there. We must be committed to God and to the man of God. Moses went up on the mount, but guess who got to go with him? His loyal apprentice, Joshua.

Joshua had prepared himself to be the servant, the one who ministered to Moses. Now, his faithfulness and loyalty in serving the man of God had separated him from the multitude. It had separated him from being just one of the boys. Was he serving as a preacher? No. He was serving Moses in menial tasks. Joshua accompanied Moses when he ascended Mount Sinai to receive the Ten Commandments. Joshua was also the first to meet Moses on his descent (Exodus 32:17). God said, *"Whosoever toucheth the mount shall be surely put to death"* (Exodus 19:12b), but Moses' servant was allowed to go where only Moses could go by reason of his relationship to Moses.

> *". . . but **his servant Joshua**, the son of Nun, a young man, departed not out of the tabernacle."*
> Exodus 33:11

Joshua was allowed to be in the tabernacle when God would come down to speak with Moses face to face. Moses had to preside in the court, but Joshua did not leave the tabernacle. He stayed in the presence of God! By serving Moses, Joshua gained benefits that otherwise would never have been his. Under the anointing and encouragement of his father-in-law, Moses had set up captains of fifties and of hundreds and of thousands (Exodus 18:13-26). It is interesting to note that when Moses died, not one of the captains who ruled over various divisions of Israel became the new leader in Israel. The position was not given to one of the hierarchy, nor to one of the religious elite. None of those captains took over the leadership — political or spiritual — of the nation. Who received the transfer of anointing? The one who had served Moses in the menial tasks. Moses imparted his anointing, his honor, and his leadership position to the loyal servant, Joshua.

> "As the LORD commanded Moses, his servant, so did Moses command Joshua, and so did Joshua; he left nothing undone of all that the LORD commanded Moses."
> Joshua 11:15

After Moses's death, Joshua's life was still a tribute to Moses. He had learned well from the master, Moses. But sadly enough, when Joshua passed from the scene, it appears that no one committed his life to Joshua in service enough to receive a transfer of the anointing. As a result, Israel slid into darkness and had to have a judge come for temporary deliverance. Perhaps no one had qualified himself to lead the nation. They apparently failed to see the apprenticeship pattern of service, unity, and loyalty. I believe that someone reading this book will learn from the life of Joshua, and will be loyal and faithful to the place of service where God has called them. I pray that God will grant us a personal revelation of "...faithful in the least — ruler over much," so that we can be the Joshuas of our generation and raise up the Joshuas for future generations.

OBEDIENCE

> "As the LORD commanded Moses, his servant, so did Moses command Joshua, and so did Joshua; he left nothing undone of all that the LORD commanded Moses."
> Joshua 11:15

Loyalty and obedience go hand in hand. If you are loyal, you are going to be obedient. Before Joshua received his own ministry, he had to learn to serve and obey Moses. Before Elisha was released into his own ministry, he had to learn to serve and obey Elijah. As in Elisha and Joshua's lives, the starting point for our ministry is going to be our "master's" revelations. We should be learning from someone who has gone on before us, not impatiently trying to get our own revelations. We can take the revelations God has already given them and build on that foundation with personal revelations that the Lord gives us. It's like getting a huge head start in a race. I would caution you, however, to know the person with whom you associate yourself. Know the fruit of the person's ministry, because you will be like them.

I reverently call Joshua 11:15 the *"We Scripture"*

because it applies to my own apprenticeship with my pastor. For example, when my pastor announces, *"We* are going to build a multi-purpose center," or "*we* are all going to go street-witnessing," I understand right from the start that *we* means *me*. If he announces under the anointing, "We're going to walk across the river...and we're not using the bridge," *we* means *me*.

Most Sunday mornings at our church we give an altar call right after the praise and worship. Nobody has even preached. We have not passed out tracts. We have done nothing but praise God, and the Spirit of God moves upon the hearts of individuals. Many people come forward in these altar calls. Do you know why? It is because the anointing flows freely where there is a willingness to serve and where there is an atmosphere of unity. It is so important to be obedient and to act on what God has shown our leader to do. The Lord will speak things to them that we may never consider otherwise. I have to admit, the first time after the praise and worship that Pastor Nichols said, "Mark, I believe God wants us to give the altar call," in the natural I thought, *"But Pastor, we haven't preached. How will they respond? What's going on here?"* But in my heart (between its rapid beats), the Spirit of God made me understand that I could do whatever Pastor Nichols asked me to do because when I submit, the anointing will flow. So if it lines up with the Word, whatever the request, we can do it. However impossible it may look, if the man

Obedience

of God under the anointing of God has requested it, I am going to be a candidate for a miracle when I obey and act in faith. Whatever God commands the man of God to do, we as a church can do.

We can look at Joshua 11:15 and use it to check our own heart regarding obedience. We ought to be able to plug our names into this Scripture, *"Norma (or whatever your name is) left nothing undone of all that God commanded her pastor to do. She was a part of the vision."* It is just like the mighty men of David in 2 Samuel 23:15-16. David mentioned, in passing, that he would like to have a drink of water from that fountain in Jerusalem. David's loyal men fought their way through enemy lines and back, risking their very lives, to get him that water. That is amazing dedication!

It puzzles me why we do not have an overabundance of workers in the church. Elisha was busy at work when Elijah found him and anointed him, at God's command, to be a prophet in his place. The workplace is where Jesus found His disciples. Today, Jesus is still looking for people who are busy doing what their "masters" have told them to do. Obedience and service are essential, yet many people are ignorant about why we serve in the church. Jesus said that if you have not been faithful in that which is another man's, who shall give you that which is your own? That is the way the anointing comes. Do not let the fact that you have a vision stop you from being part of your pastor's vision. Do not let "your calling" stop you from serving the man of God. The man of God has some things that you need. Why should we reinvent the wheel when we already have a prime opportunity, with a wealth of experience in God, set right in front of our eyes? Why not plug into what God is already doing?

The Bible says that if you cannot love your brother whom you see, you cannot love God whom you do not see (1 John 4:20). I say that if you cannot serve the man of God that you see, you cannot, in the fullest sense, serve God. We start out first in the natural and then move into the spiritual. Our natural lives can be a serious indicator of our spiritual lives. The worldly view of authority or leadership is one who is in authority, but the biblical view is always one who is *under* authority.

> *"...but whosoever will be great among you, let him be your minister; And whosoever will be chief among you, let him be your servant: Even as the Son of man came not to be ministered unto, but to minister, and to give his life a ransom for many."*
>
> Matthew 20:26-28

Jesus said that the rulers of the Gentiles lord it over them, but the real leader who is trained under the man of God is always *under* authority. There is safety and protection under authority. The apprentice learns to serve and to submit and, because he is faithful in those areas, he is promoted. Then he begins to move on to other areas

Obedience

where he is flowing in the anointing that God has placed upon him.

Every believer should have a spiritual authority — a pastor — to whom they are personally accountable. If we are having trouble with authority here in this earth, we do not have a full understanding of authority. If we cannot personally submit to and obey authority, we will never be trusted with a position of authority in God's kingdom.

BEING A "PASTOR'S FRIEND"

Being a "pastor's friend" is another old-time colloquialism that isn't used very much these days. A pastor's friend is someone who is supportive. I think of those "I Like Ike" buttons that people wore during the Dwight D. Eisenhower presidential campaign. How many of those button-wearing people actually knew Eisenhower personally? That wasn't the point. They were supporters. When I refer to "pastor" I am especially referring to the pastor of the church, but it also applies to any person in leadership whom we have been called to serve, whether it be in the church or a secular job. Part of serving our pastor is being a friend or supporter to them. A friend is *someone who is attached to another by affection or esteem; one that is not hostile; and sometimes a favored companion*. Not everyone will be a close personal friend of the pastor, but we can all be faithful to support him.

We are to esteem those who have sown into our lives to help us grow and mature in the Lord, and to be faithful where God has planted us. The Word says that we are to love and respect our pastor. Someone who loves the

Spiritual Apprenticeship

pastor doesn't expose his faults to others. Nor do they murmur and complain about him.

> *"A talebearer revealeth secrets: but he that is of a faithful spirit concealeth the matter."*
> Proverbs 11:13

> *"... And Ham, the father of Canaan, saw the nakedness of his father, and told his two brethren without. And Shem and Japheth took a garment, and laid it upon both their shoulders, and went backward, and covered the nakedness of their father; and their faces were backward, and they saw not their father's nakedness."*
> Genesis 9:22-23

Canaan saw Noah's nakedness and exposed him to others. Shem and Japheth covered their father and were blessed because of it. Love covers a multitude of sins.

> *"These six things doth the L*ord *hate: yea, seven are an abomination unto him: A proud look, a lying tongue, and hands that shed innocent blood, An heart that deviseth wicked imaginations, feet that be swift in running to mischief, A false witness that speaketh lies,* **and he that soweth discord among brethren***."*
> Proverbs 6:16-19

If we see a fault in our pastor, it is our duty to pray for them, not to gossip or sow seeds of division. One of the problems of today is when people don't understand something that the pastor says or does, and they start griping about it among their friends. They don't realize that they are hurting themselves and preventing the fullness of God from operating in their lives. The Bible tells us that whatever we sow into someone else's life will come back into our own. This can work to our advantage, but it will work against us if we're sowing strife and contention.

Korah's Rebellion

Not only should we refuse to be offended, but we must refuse to take up someone else's offense against leadership or anyone else. Some people will get their feelings hurt. They become offended and will leave the church because of something that was said to them. They may even convince others to leave with them, saying, "God led me to leave and go over to another church." That is not true. *God will never lead anyone by means of an offense.* If God is calling you to another church, it will be with peace, not through strife or offense. The Bible shows us how God views strife and the undermining of authority. Numbers 16 and Numbers 26:9-11 give us the account of Korah and his cohorts, Dathan, Abiram and On. They gathered with two hundred-fifty other prominent leaders of Israel and rebelled against the authority of Moses and Aaron. It is important to remember that when someone strives against leadership, they are really striving against God. Remember, He is the One who sets up all authority.

"Let every soul be subject unto the higher powers. For there is no power but of God: the powers that be are ordained of God. Whosoever therefore resisteth the power,

> *resisteth the ordinance of God: and they that resist shall receive to themselves damnation."*
>
> Romans 13:1-2

Korah went before Moses and Aaron saying, *"Who do you think you are? We are the people of God, just like you are. What right do you have to act as though you are different than any of us?"* Instead of being grateful for all that Moses had done, laying down his very life for them, they wanted to overthrow him. They had the telltale signs of rebellion.

> *"Seemeth it but a small thing unto you, that the God of Israel hath separated you from the congregation of Israel, to bring you near to himself to do the service of the tabernacle of the LORD, and to stand before the congregation to minister unto them? And he hath brought thee near to him, and all thy brethren the sons of Levi with thee: and seek ye the priesthood also? For which cause **both thou and all thy company are gathered together against the LORD:** and what is Aaron, that ye murmur against him?"*
>
> Numbers 16:9-11

Moses was shocked that Korah and those who stood with him failed to appreciate their position on God's team. Again, instead of being *grateful* that God had counted them as special to care for the Tabernacle that housed the presence of God, they thought the grass looked greener on the priesthood side of the fence. They were not content to be what God called them to be. They felt confined or trapped and looked at their position as being demeaning or inferior to someone else's position.

Nothing was farther from the truth! Korah and his followers became so envious of someone else's position, that they decided to take action to promote themselves for the "higher" position.

It is a privilege and honor to serve, whether it be in the nursery, cleaning the restrooms, or in the pulpit. There is nothing new under the sun. Even today there are people who are not satisfied in doing what God has called them to do. They gripe and complain that they should be preaching in the pulpit or have a position with a "title" instead of changing diapers in the nursery. What they fail to understand is that even if they are called to one day have a pulpit ministry, until they are faithful in the preparation stages — which may include changing diapers for a few years — they will not have God's full anointing or blessing on their ministry. Even worse, they may even become castaways. The worst thing would be to be promoted without being prepared. Impartation is part of preparation and impartation can take time. You don't get it all in one day!

God has established leadership in the church. Moses acknowledged that his authority came from God and not of himself (Numbers 16:28). Moses said, *"Okay, you want to offer incense? Go ahead and do as you please. We'll see what God has to say about it."*

"And the earth opened her mouth, and swallowed them up, and their houses, and all the men that apper-

> tained unto Korah, and all their goods. They, and all that appertained to them, went down alive into the pit, and the earth closed upon them: and they perished from among the congregation."
>
> Numbers 16:32-33

Despite warnings, these people went ahead and did things their own way. God made His point clear. The earth opened up and swallowed those who refused to submit to the authority that God put in place. Rebellion cost Korah his life.

> "And there came out a fire from the LORD, and consumed the two hundred and fifty men that offered incense."
>
> Numbers 16:35

God gave the other 250 people the opportunity to separate themselves from Korah and the rebellion, but they didn't break away. Those who took up Korah's offense were also destroyed. Great fire came down from heaven and consumed them. Those that were burning the "strange fire" were themselves killed by fire.

> "...Touch not mine anointed, and do my prophets no harm."
>
> 1 Chronicles 16:22

God takes exception to those who try to usurp the authority that He has set up.

Remember, no attempt to usurp authority will ever be blessed.

You would think that after the ground swallowing one group of rebels and fire consuming others that the children of Israel would have gotten the point, but they didn't! They again took up an offense, murmuring and blaming Moses and Aaron for the deaths of the rebels! Fourteen thousand, seven hundred people died from the plague that was birthed from that offense.

> *"And Aaron took as Moses commanded, and ran into the midst of the congregation; and, behold, the plague was begun among the people: and he put on incense, and made an atonement for the people. And he stood between the dead and the living; and the plague was stayed."*
> Numbers 16:47-48

Moses and Aaron could have just given up and said, *"They have it coming! Look at what a pain they've been!"* But they didn't. They fell on their faces and prayed to God on behalf of the people! That is the heart of a godly leader. They intercede, even when the people don't deserve it.

Sowing and Reaping is a Law that Works

Just as God will deal with those who do not honor authority, He will also bless and prosper those who do. The law of sowing and reaping always works.

> *"Let him that is taught in the word communicate unto him that teacheth in all good things. Be not deceived; God is not mocked: for whatsoever a man soweth, that shall he also reap. For he that soweth to his flesh shall of the flesh reap corruption; but he that soweth to the Spirit shall of the Spirit reap life everlasting. And let us not be weary in well doing: for in due season we shall reap, if we faint not. As we have therefore opportunity, let us do good unto all*

men, especially unto them who are of the household of faith."

Galatians 6:6-10

We need to look for opportunities to serve and bless our pastor out of love for him, not because we expect special privileges or kickbacks in return. Often times people are willing to serve, but they have strings attached. "I'll help pastor out, but I'd better get a special seat for those meetings." What is our motive? Who are we serving? Are we serving to get glory from man? We need to learn to serve as unto the Lord and cut the strings.

> *"Withhold not good from them to whom it is due, when it is in the power of thine hand to do it."*
>
> Proverbs 3:27

> *"Render therefore to all their dues: tribute to whom tribute is due; custom to whom custom; fear to whom fear; honour to whom honour."*
>
> Romans 13:7

> *"Let the elders that rule well be counted worthy of double honour, especially they who labour in the word and doctrine."*
>
> 1 Timothy 5:17

Special Occasions

It is important for us to give honor to whom honor is due. Pastors lay down their lives for the people they serve. They work long hard hours for their congregations. Many people would be shocked if they could see all a pastor has to deal with in the course of a day or week behind the scenes. We need to show appreciation for them. Honor them on special days like birthdays or anniversaries. Many people have never thought about it, but pastors are people and need encouragement just like we do. Do you appreciate gifts and surprises? A pastor cannot very well stand up and take a special offering for his own birthday, so we need to be the one to spearhead that cause.

Appreciation doesn't always have to have a high price tag, though there are times that do warrant that. Send them a card or a special note and tell them how they have blessed your life. Find out their favorite restaurant and get them a gift certificate. There are many things you can do that can put a little pep in their step and a glide in their stride. We should make it our duty to make them smile. And don't forget their spouse! They need love too!

Bless Their Children

"His seed shall be mighty upon earth: the generation of the upright shall be blessed."
Psalm 112:2

"The children of thy servants shall continue, and their seed shall be established before thee."
Psalm 102:28

Another good way to sow into your pastor's life is to honor his children. Many times people don't realize the challenges that come with being a minister's child. Bless them without any regard for your own personal gain.

Remember, what you make happen for someone else's house, God will make happen for your house.

Pray for Those in Authority

> *"I exhort therefore, that, first of all, supplications, prayers, intercessions, and giving of thanks, be made for all men; For kings, and for all that are in authority; that we may lead a quiet and peaceable life in all godliness and honesty. For this is good and acceptable in the sight of God our Saviour."*
>
> 1 Timothy 2:1-3

Most importantly, keep your pastor lifted up in prayer. Specifically pray that God would give them wisdom and discernment. Pray for protection over them and their families. It has never been more important than it is right now to keep our leader's hands lifted like Aaron and Hur did for Moses in Exodus 17:11-12. As long as our leaders have people lifting them up, they can continue to win the battles that they must face. When we do not lift them up, we ourselves become part of the casualties. We need to take our places as loyal members on the team where God has placed us. United we stand, divided we fall.

11

BEWARE OF EXCESSES

Jesus said it first (Luke 16:12) and I cannot improve on it:

If you have not been faithful in someone else's ministry, you cannot have your own ministry.

That is why we must use extreme caution, wisdom and discernment when joining ourselves to anyone.

Most of the staff ministers where I am on staff have been here for years. The reason is because the pastor, Pastor Bob Nichols, is a man of integrity who has a proven track record of trustworthiness which spans decades. It is a mutually beneficial relationship. He pours into us, and we are trusted to wholeheartedly serve in our positions on the team. We can serve him, unhindered, because he has earned the respect we have for him. I have heard unfortunate testimonies of other places where the leader/staff relationships were not as positive, in fact they are quite the opposite. That negative type of situation needs to be addressed.

Spiritual Apprenticeship

Sometimes leaders have failed God, and some have openly rebelled. David and Samuel both served men who failed God. Even so, both of these men went on to fulfill their calls from God. David served Saul, a king who had lost his position because of disobedience and pride. David did not let Saul's failure stop him from operating in the anointing. He served with a heart of submission, and continued to do what was right. Samuel served Eli, a man who chose to honor his sons more than he honored the Lord. Eli refused to take strong action when his sons were being a reproach to the name of the Lord. But, Samuel did not let that stop him from doing what was right. David and Samuel did not let the failure of their masters cause them to fail in their own lives. If our eyes are on Jesus, He will put in us the good things, the anointing, and we will bypass failure. We will even learn from the mistakes of others and be able to advance if we refuse to let bitterness or pride kill our spiritual growth. Receive what your teachers know and make that knowledge the launching pad for ministry, allowing the Word of God to grow within you as you do what is right in the sight of the Lord.

> *"Be ye not unequally yoked together with unbelievers: for what fellowship hath righteousness with unrighteousness? and what communion hath light with darkness?"*
> 2 Corinthians 6:14

Although this Scripture is often applied to marriage, we need to be sure that we do not become unequally yoked in *any* relationship. I have heard our pastor say,

"If you don't pray going in, you'll pray to get out." That is why we must constantly stay in close fellowship with the Holy Spirit and pray for God's guidance in our relationships.

Apprenticeship is NOT the same as "The Shepherding Movement"

Some may confuse the teaching of spiritual apprenticeship with the excess of control that was found in the Shepherding Movement. Apprenticeship does not seek *control*, but rather seeks to train, develop and *discipline* apprentices to be strong in the Lord on their own, and to better exercise their anointing. It is simple to identify the difference between the motivations of *discipline* versus *control*.

- With *discipline*, the motive is to establish strength in the apprentice that will equip him or her to succeed *on their own*.

- *Control* seeks to have someone else depend on *them* rather than on Jesus Christ. The apprentice is manipulated for selfish reasons rather than being given every opportunity to develop their own maturity and strength.

The difference between apprenticeship and shepherding is like the difference between adoption and slavery.

Spiritual Apprenticeship

The motive of a leader in a godly apprenticeship relationship is not to establish control over the apprentice, but to nurture growth and maturity as a spiritual father or mother. Jesus is our model for relationships. His motive with us is genuine love and concern for our best interest. The same should be true for every leader. Jesus laid down His life for His disciples and served them. He poured His life into getting *them* prepared to get the job done. He entrusted the evangelization of the entire known world into their hands. The disciples realized the love Jesus had for them and the sacrifice He made. He earned their love and respect to the point that rather than renounce Him, they were martyred for Him.

A godly leader does not command people to believe that *they* are the source of security. Neither do they demand that people become dependent solely on them. That is abusive. If anyone finds themselves under that type of situation, they need to get out immediately. If a godly leader sees that someone is becoming dependent upon them, they certainly do not encourage it. A godly authority figure will offer suggestions and help train and equip someone to make their own decisions, not mandate every move they make.

I have heard of situations where people sold everything they had and uprooted their families to go to a foreign country as missionaries solely on a "word of prophecy" from their leader. They never had a desire to

Beware of Excesses

go, nor had the thought ever crossed their minds prior to the "word." Let me tell you, if you get a word like that and it isn't confirmation of something God has already put in your heart, DON'T GO. These people did not seek God for themselves. They ran off only to return a few months later sick, weary and financially destitute. While we should seek godly counsel before getting married, I have heard of people who entered into an arranged marriage with someone they didn't even know merely on the word of an ungodly leader. Now these same people are trying to piece together the shreds of their torn lives because they submitted themselves to a selfish or foolish person without seeking God.

A godly leader will never use anyone merely for their own convenience. I know of a minister who constantly volunteered his assistant for things with absolutely no regard for the assistant. It was as if he were a slave rather than assistant. On one occasion the assistant was volunteered to help some people move. The assistant was treated with such love and respect by these people that it shocked him. He shouldn't have been shocked. He should always have been treated with love and respect, especially by his "boss." A good leader seeks to serve, not just to be served. He also treats the people who work with him with respect, love and courtesy.

A good leader will allow the people on his team to use their gifts and callings without excessive scrutiny. My pastor has given his staff the freedom to operate their departments without someone constantly watching over their shoulders. We each know our role and the pastor trusts us to do our jobs with excellence and integrity. It is a trust that has been mutually earned.

Shirking Responsibility

An unhealthy relationship can also occur when a person refuses to take responsibility for making his own decisions regarding important personal matters. Godly counsel is when someone sits down with their authority figure to look at the different options and to pray for God's guidance on which option to choose. I know of people who say they want to come in for counsel, when really they just want me to tell them what to do. People sometimes do that because if it doesn't work out, they want to have someone else to blame. After all is said and done, the decision is up to that individual, not me. Godly leaders encourage people to get into the Word for themselves and to develop their own walk with God so they can make good choices.

How can we avoid excessive and abusive relationships? Jesus said *"My sheep hear my voice, and I know them, and they follow me"* (John 10:27). We need to discern the voice of God to get our direction from Him. We do this through the Holy Spirit by the Word of God. The more time we spend in the Word with Him, the more sensitive we become to His voice. We cannot trust only our brains or emotions to lead us.

> *"For as the heavens are higher than the earth, so are my ways higher than your ways, and my thoughts than your thoughts. For as the rain cometh down, and the snow from heaven, and returneth not thither, but watereth the earth, and maketh it bring forth and bud, that it may give seed to the sower, and bread to the eater: So shall my word be that goeth forth out of my mouth: it shall not return unto me void, but it shall accomplish that which I please, and it shall prosper in the thing whereto I sent it. For ye shall go out with joy, and be led forth with peace."*
>
> Isaiah 55:9-12

The best way to avoid abuse and excess is to stay in consistent fellowship with Him. He will show us all we need to know. He will send us out with joy and lead us with peace. He will guide us into the right relationships. We just have to listen.

FAITHFULNESS IN LITTLE THINGS WILL LAUNCH YOU INTO BIG THINGS

Often times when people think of ministry, they think limelight, success, wealth and glory. But, God shows us again and again that He sees ministry as service — running errands, attending to another, doing the menial tasks. What did Jesus say He came to do?

> *"Even as the Son of man came not to be ministered unto, but to minister, and to give his life a ransom for many."*
>
> Matthew 20:28

Verses 25-27 urge us to follow His example:

> *"But Jesus called them unto him, and said, Ye know that the princes of the Gentiles exercise dominion over them, and they that are great exercise authority upon them. But it shall not be so among you: but whosoever will be great among you, let him be your minister; And whosoever will be chief among you, let him be your servant."*
>
> Matthew 20:25-27

Jesus demonstrated this service.

> *"He riseth from supper, and laid aside his garments; and took a towel and girded himself. After that he poureth water into a basin, and began to wash the disciples' feet, and to wipe them with the towel wherewith he was girded... So after he had washed their feet, and had taken his garments, and was set down again, he said unto them, Know ye what I have done to you? Ye call me Master and LORD: and ye say well; for so I am. If I then, your LORD and Master, have washed your feet; ye also ought to wash one another's feet. For I have given you an example, that ye should do as I have done to you. Verily, verily, I say unto you, the servant is not greater than his lord; neither he that is sent greater than he that sent him."*
>
> John 13:4-5, 12-16

As I meditated on this, I understood that God, the Word made Flesh, demonstrated service in the lowliest task. If God did that for the disciples, we ought to serve one another, not necessarily in a foot-washing ceremony but in any task, even the lowly ones, that glorify God.

It is simply stated in Psalm 75:6-7 that promotion comes not from man, but from God. It does not come from the east, the west, or the south. God is the one who puts one down and sets another up. Promotion is the result of a transfer of anointing which always follows a life of surrender and submission.

Some may throw the word "anointing" around indiscriminately, as though it means nothing. But to those of us who have experienced it, the anointing that comes in the presence of God is the most precious aspect of the ministry, so much so that we actively seek its transfer.

> *"Humble yourselves therefore under the mighty hand of God, that he may exalt you in due time."*
>
> 1 Peter 5:6

When we put God's kingdom first and decide we are going to advance His kingdom whether or not we ever receive recognition, whether or not we are ever in the limelight, that is *humility*. Spiritual apprenticeship builds a relationship of accountability that is rooted in humility and obedience. The intensive nurturing of a godly apprenticeship greatly speeds the growth of the individual being apprenticed. It also teaches submission to delegated authority by eliminating pride. This is a foundational principle in the Word of God. Commitment to serving God first gives the apprenticeship the proper perspective. Some folks have seen abuses in authority (we went over that in the previous chapter), but it is wrong to throw the baby out with the bath water. We must remember that submission to authority is not just a suggestion. It is an imperative in the Word of God.

People are frequently tempted to step beyond the anointing God has placed on their lives, or to step out of God's timing and order. In doing so they attempt to press into an office for which they are not equipped. The things of the Spirit come as He wills, not as we will. Walking in His fullness will come only as we do things His way.

Spiritual Apprenticeship

You will never grow beyond your willingness to serve. In the body of Christ, the servants are the promotable ones.

Those who are not afraid to serve those in authority are being prepared by God to bear authority.

When you are willing to start where you are with what you have, however small, you are on your way to spiritual growth.

For many years the door that was open to me for service was music, in particular playing the drums. Even though all I held in my hand was a drumstick, I knew if I would be faithful to invest what I had, God would be faithful to multiply it. The diligence that it takes to attend praise and worship rehearsals and to be at all the services was great training. It also gave me the opportunity to experience the anointing of many great men and women of God from one of the best seats in the house.

Somewhere along the line it was ingrained in me that in order to be promotable you need to be faithful. To be faithful meant doing whatever your hands found to do and to do it with all your heart as unto the Lord. There is something about being faithful *when no one else is looking* that God really loves. That is where real character develops. I remember one music minister I served under. He would call Sunday morning rehearsals for 8:30 or 9:00 almost every week. I don't remember anyone ever coming, with the exception of the drummer (me) and a soundman. Some may consider it foolish to show up with such a low turnout, but I choose to consider it radical faithfulness. That is the kind of faithfulness that serves as unto the Lord, regardless of the applause of man. God was faithful to expand that seed I planted, and eventually it grew to be its own music ministry. For several years God used music as a platform for me to reach out to teenagers and to prepare me for full-time ministry. Service to God is a seed that will grow only when planted. Service to God will always work with established godly authority to benefit the body of Christ, rather than working for selfish gain.

As it turned out, one Sunday morning, while I was just being faithful to play those drums, Pastor Bob Nichols went to the pulpit with a need for a youth minister. The Lord spoke to him and told him that his youth-ministry man was seated right behind him! Later, when I found this out, I quietly rejoiced that I had stuck it out and remained faithful. My destiny was tied up in being faithful to what some might consider insignificant.

Everything you are doing today is preparation for the ultimate plan God has for your life.

Your destiny lies on the other side of your diligence in school or secular employment. Never let the great things you want to do for God keep you from being faithful in the small things He has given you today.

There were times when it seemed that God would never bring me to the place of ministry I desired. Other young people I knew were finding open doors to ministry or were even taking staff positions. It seemed that nothing would ever move for me. There were times I complained to the Lord, arguing that I was more qualified or even had a deeper walk with Him than those others did. It can be discouraging, even heartbreaking, to feel left behind or left out. The worst thing you can do when you are believing for promotion is to give up. You could be moments away from your breakthrough!

> *"And let us not be weary in well doing: for in due season we shall reap, if we faint not."*
> Galatians 6:9

After all the faithfulness you have sown and the time you have invested, you can't quit. You are closer than you have ever been! Do not quit; do not give up; do not be moved by delay. Your promotion is on the way. The deeper your foundation, the higher you can build.

> *"For God is not unrighteous to forget your work and labor of love, which ye have shewed toward his name, in that ye have ministered to the saints, and do minister."*
> Hebrews 6:10

It is a privilege to serve anywhere in the body of Christ. Be patient and take the time to build strong character. Do whatever you can for God and do it the best you can. Others may seem to be passing you by. They may seem to be getting promotions and attention, but don't worry about them. You do what's right because it's right, and keep doing it. If they have not laid the foundations of faithfulness and service, you will pass them going the other way.

ENCOURAGEMENT TO THOSE SEEKING PROMOTION

Promotion in the spiritual realm is not about place or position, but about character and integrity. These things are available to every believer regardless of title or office. A fully developed anointing and character are within your grasp. In the final analysis, the person dying of cancer does not care if you are the senior pastor or a plumber. They only want to know if you can help them get their need met. Is it your desire to have the anointing operative in your life so that you can connect them with God's healing power? *You can get there from here.*

This desire comes even more as we come into relationship with men and women of God who know God better than we do. Someone has said that the two greatest agents for change in our lives are the books we read and the people we know. They challenge and encourage us to know that if they did it, we can, too. Because God is no respecter of persons (Acts 10:34), if they can receive promotion, so can we. Since we become like our friends, I want friends who challenge me to know and love God better. Friendships are good, but we also need to have someone speak into our life as a leader — one who has been where we haven't yet been and will share what they have learned with us. We need to have an apprenticeship relationship with a more mature, well-seasoned person who is walking in the wisdom of God. It will be easy to ask them questions, such as, *How would you handle this? What do you think about this? What does this Scripture mean?* The words of a man, Proverbs 18:4 says, are as a deep stream, also:

> "Counsel in the heart of man is like deep water; but a man of understanding will draw it out."
>
> Proverbs 20:5

A person of wisdom will learn how to draw out of that stream. Are you at ease with your superiors, or with those who are more mature? We need to use wisdom in choosing who we associate with on a regular basis. I want to be around people who are filled with the love of God, refreshed in the Lord, and have a hunger to go higher with God, not around those who are burned out, tainted by things they have seen, or defiled by bitterness and resentment. Even more so, I want to link up in a close personal relationship with a seasoned veteran of the Lord to learn from them, one on one. I want to learn from those of good character and integrity. I have found that in these relationships we need to listen and observe more than we speak because they have a lot of wisdom to impart to us.

Encouragement To Those Seeking Promotion

God has a lot more invested in them than we could ever imagine. If we observe how things are handled and how people are treated, we will really gain an insight for our lives from the people that we esteem. We can obtain intensive training by learning from their wealth of experience in the things of God and by the Word operating in their lives on a day to day basis.

There is always more with God. There are higher levels of anointing and deeper levels of intimacy with Him. There are also various levels of service in the things of God. Remember, it is a privilege to serve, no matter what the capacity, but let me offer some encouragement and instructions for those who desire promotion.

Responsibilities & tasks will be delegated to you before you're given authority.

God does not usually call people who think waiting on God is sitting still and doing nothing. You may think, sometimes, a task is just busywork, *"You know, I'm called to preach, and here I am sweeping this hall."* Let me remind you from 1 Kings 19:16, that God told Elijah to anoint Elisha as prophet in his same position. Immediately, Elijah went out and obeyed God. From that point on the calling was there for Elisha, but he did not begin to prophesy; he began to do the laundry. He was still called, he was going to be the prophet, but he had to stick with Elijah and do the things he requested. We can read in 2 Kings 2 that because of his faithfulness to the man of God, Elisha got to write his own ticket, telling Elijah exactly what he wanted.

Paul wrote many times that certain ones had forsaken him. About one he said, *"Demas hath forsaken me, having loved this present world"* (2 Timothy 4:10). But to Timothy who was faithful, he said, "I'm willing to train you, and God is going to do great things in your life." Jesus chose Judas Iscariot to enter into this same kind of apprenticeship relationship, yet Judas chose to betray Jesus. We may be called, but we still have to make the choice to "do the stuff."

I cannot think of a much better example of God honoring a servant (other than Jesus) than Stephen. In Acts 6:1-6 we read that he was a man full of the Holy Ghost and wisdom who was chosen, basically, to wait on tables. He was a true servant. He made sure that he tended to his assigned menial tasks. But, look at Acts 6:8 . . . .

> *"And Stephen, full of faith and power, did great wonders and miracles among the people."*
>
> Acts 6:8

Stephen focused on serving with all of his heart, and God granted supernatural power. When he was martyred for Christ, we see the beautiful heart of a true servant of God. He actually prayed for his murderers (Acts 7:55-60). Stephen was a man full of faith and power, a man who waited on tables. When he answered the call, he did everything that he was called to do, not just the "limelight" tasks.

To be one that answers the call, you need to understand that you will be delegated tasks before you are ever given authority. So be satisfied, knowing that he who is faithful in that which is the least is faithful also in much. The testing ground for spiritual authority is whether you are faithful in that which is the least.

You need to prove your faithfulness over time.

Anyone can look good for thirty to ninety days, but a spiritual apprenticeship develops over the long haul, day in and day out, year in and year out. Often times apprenticeships are long. Beginning in about 1630, a legal apprenticeship was to be for a seven-year period. The apostle Paul was in the desert for thirteen years, training for ministry. Jesus trained thirty years for a three-and-a-half-year ministry. Long apprenticeships are more often the case than not. We will get to minister along the way, but God is preparing us for specific callings. We must not shortcut our time of preparation. Toward the end of his long life and ministry I heard that a minister once said, "If I knew I had twenty-two years to accomplish my assigned task here on the earth, I'd spend twenty of those years preparing for it." We prove our faithfulness over the long haul through our perseverance.

Spiritual Apprenticeship

Remember, Elisha was not the first servant that Elijah had. When he believed God on Mount Carmel for rain, Elijah sent the servant to check for rain seven times. The servant said, "Oh, there's just a cloud the size of a man's hand. There isn't anything out there. We're wasting our time praying." This servant was not Elisha. This was another servant. This was a faithless, unspiritual servant, one who walked out, so to speak, because as soon as the Mount Carmel experience was over, Elijah said to him, "You wait over here in this town. I'm going over there." We never hear about this servant again. Elijah never went back to pick him up. Why? Because he was faithless. He washed out. He was doubting, unfaithful, disloyal, and unspiritual. He did not answer the call of God on his life. God gave Elijah someone else to train in his place who would be faithful and receive the double portion anointing.

As we discussed earlier, Elijah told Elisha the same thing he had told the faithless servant. "You tarry here in this city while I go over across the river." Elisha's response was, "No way! I'm staying with you."

> *"And it came to pass, when they were gone over, that Elijah said unto Elisha, Ask what I shall do for thee, before I be taken away from thee. And Elisha said, I pray thee, let a double portion of thy spirit be upon me. And he said, Thou hast asked a hard thing: nevertheless, if thou see me when I am taken from thee, it shall be so unto thee;*

but if not, it shall not be so. And it came to pass, as they still went on, and talked, that, behold, there appeared a chariot of fire, and horses of fire, and parted them both asunder; and Elijah went up by a whirlwind into heaven. And Elisha saw it..."

2 Kings 2:9-12

Because Elisha had been faithful to stay with him, Elijah asked what he could do for him. Elisha asked for a double portion of the anointing that was on Elijah. Elijah told him, "If you stick with me until the very end, you'll have it!" He did, and he got it! The Bible declares that there were exactly twice as many miracles recorded in Elisha's life as there were in Elijah's.

Realize that a real man or woman of God will lay hands on no man suddenly.

Now what does that mean? It means that a man or woman of God is not going to ordain you or pull you into the ministry immediately. He or she knows that it takes time to prove faithfulness in small things before you can qualify. But you can guarantee that if you are faithful and patient, God is speaking to somebody about taking you under their care, to teach and train you.

"Servants, be obedient to them that are your masters according to the flesh, with fear and trembling, in singleness of your heart, as unto Christ; not with eyeservice as menpleasers; but as the servants of Christ, doing the will of God from the heart; with good will doing service, as to

the LORD, *and not to men: knowing that whatsoever good thing any man doeth, the same shall he receive of the* LORD, *whether he be bond or free."*

Ephesians 6:5

When an apprentice had completed his training, he was called a free man. *A free man!* In today's vernacular that verse would read, "Whether you are still in that time of apprenticeship or whether you are a free man and you have received promotion into the things of God, always do this kind of service as unto the Lord, whether or not somebody is looking. Be faithful and diligent because there is going to be a reward."

Do you know what that reward is? You get to be with Jesus. You get to develop a personal relationship with Him. The whole concept between our being in a right relationship with our teachers, or with our pastor, or with a mature man or woman of God is not so that we can be like them, although we will be, but so there will be a transfer of anointing. The real heart of this message is, *how do I become more like God?* How do I increase my personal relationship with Jesus?

The Bible is clear. You do not need any man to teach you, John says in 1 John 2:27, because the same anointing abides in you. You do not *have* to have teachers if none are available, but God's *best* plan *is* to have an apprenticeship relationship through which we can learn, hands on, from someone who has "been there, done that." In the list of gifts to the Body of Christ, He mentions teachers.

Encouragement To Those Seeking Promotion

You could be a Paul in the desert, but eventually Paul had Barnabas who tutored him. Paul went beyond that relationship with Barnabas, and began to impart to others himself.

I want to be a minister of God, one who can receive direct commands and direct tasks from God. How do I get there from here? I may not always be as successful in gleaning that from the Word, but if I can find someone who knows God more than I do, I can learn from the relationship with God that they have. When I find someone whose relationship, prayer life, and understanding of the Word are strong, I want them to lay hands on me, spend time with me, and teach me. Why? Because they know things that I don't know, things I need to know. So I pray, "Lord, help us today, give us those divine appointments, show us who to connect with so that we can get closer to you, because we want to be like you."

Developing that closer walk with the Lord is the goal of the apprentice relationship. Promotion comes to you not because of man, even though God often uses man to bring it to pass. It comes from God. God is shaping you through schooling. He is causing you to be prepared for promotion. I encourage you to serve faithfully. Joshua's job was to do everything that God commanded Moses to do. Unless you are willing to do faithfully, from the heart, what God commands someone else, you will not be promotable. Favor will be the by-product of service.

Favor is going to manifest itself in more responsibility. If you have favor from someone who is in authority, they are going to trust you and entrust tasks to you. Many times people think of favor in the selfish light of recognition: *I'll get recognized. I'll get honored. I'll get a raise.* Recognition should not be our motive. The primary motive is to please God and to be a blessing to someone else. Do not ever be in a place where you are not serving because service is what opens the door of promotion.

GETTING ON A CHURCH STAFF AND STAYING

The highest level of spiritual growth available to the believer is *not* being in full-time ministry. God will judge us for what *He* has called us to do, in whatever particular field that may be. Therefore, the highest call is to do exactly what *He* wills. Obedience to what *He* directs us to do is the mark we need to press on toward. However, since there are those who will read this book who *are* called to serve on a church staff, it will benefit us to look at what it takes to get on and stay on the team.

The simple truth is that *you will never make a better minister than you are a Christian.* The strength of a minister's effectiveness will always be his or her personal walk with God. The basics of a growing prayer life and a daily time in God's Word will never be outgrown. Beyond this there are several truths that will help you get on the team and stay there. Please understand that this is not some formula or recipe. These are merely some observations I have made through the years of my life.

Getting on the Team:

1. ***Understand that ministry is work.*** Many times people don't realize how much administrative work it takes behind the scenes to put a man in the pulpit for 45 minutes. Your entire perspective of ministry has to change if you wonder what people could possibly keep busy doing between Sundays. The ministry is more than preaching; it is helping people. Helping people takes a lot of work. As a minister you must be willing to do what it takes to get the job done.

2. ***Learn to be a self-starter.*** Make yourself available to serve and finish the jobs that are given to you. Do not be choosy. Be willing to serve in whatever capacity is needed even if it is not in the area you feel called. Be self-motivated, someone that leadership does not have to baby-sit. It takes faith to do what you are asked to do because you may not always think that you are able. The Lord once told a friend of mine, *"Stretch real good, or else you'll pull a muscle."* Stretch and you will grow. Trust that leadership can sometimes see ability in you that you do not see.

3. ***Dress sharp.*** Do the best you can with what you have. While the Lord does not judge by outward appearance, people do. Right or wrong, how you present yourself makes a difference. The church is looking at you as a possible representative, so dress the part. Dress

for what you want to become and do not be surprised if people begin to treat you as such. You are a representative of the Lord in both conduct and appearance, so do your best.

4. ***Have a heart for the leader.*** The hireling desires promotion for selfish purposes. Leaders need team players who have a heart for them, as well as for the ministry. Learn to honor the man of God and you will be blessed. Treat him like you want to be treated and you will be enacting the law of sowing and reaping. Sow respect and honor, and you will reap the same.

Staying on the Team:

1. ***Get a word from God.*** Know that it is God's will for you to be on this particular staff and be determined to stick with it. Having a word from the Lord will keep you steady through the ups and downs.

2. ***Do not be distracted by the human element.*** When you see mistakes or flaws in your leader or another team member, do not be distracted. Rather, cover them in prayer. We all need mercy. Many times what we do not understand would become clear to us if we had all the information they had.

3. ***Provide solutions.*** Be a part of the answer, not the problem. Anyone can identify a problem; be the one that fixes it. Overcome obstacles and do not be stopped

by them. Obstacles are only temporary hurdles. Purpose not to leave any job unfinished.

4. **Be thankful.** *Refuse to focus on the negative.* Instead, be thankful that things are as good as they are. Do not allow the devil to cause you to forget the things you love about your job (95 percent) in favor of complaining about the small percentage (5 percent) of things you dislike. Keep choosing to rejoice about what is right.

5. ***Know when to shut up and when to shout.*** There is a time to be silent and a time to speak up. Pray for discernment to know the difference. Joshua at the battle of Jericho (See Joshua 6) knew the spiritual power of the shout of unity. When we shout together, the enemy's defenses fall flat.

6. ***Do not expect to always be treated like a sheep when you are on the leadership team.*** The leader's job is to minister to the sheep. Matthew 20:28 says, *"Even as the Son of man came not to be ministered unto, but to minister, and to give his life a ransom for many."* A leadership position is not a position in which you are to be coddled.

7. **Make the leader's priority yours.** We've gone over this verse again and again, but it bears repeating. Luke 16:12, *"And if ye have not been faithful in that which is another man's, who shall give you that which is your own?"*

ATTITUDES THAT BLOCK PROMOTION

Philippians 3:14 says that we are to, *"...press toward the mark for the prize of the high calling of God in Christ Jesus."* That means we are to press on for promotion in the things of God. The following attitudes will block promotion, but not necessarily in this order of importance or significance.

Jealousy

Jealousy is one of the first things to block promotion because we will not usually serve someone, from our heart, if we are jealous of them. If we want to see success, we will learn from that person, rather than be jealous of them. We will love them. Love always looks for the good in people. A wise person will put down jealousy because jealousy is envy. James 3:16 says that wherever envy and strife are, there is every evil work — not every good work but every evil work. We want our lives to reflect good work.

Stubbornness

Being stubborn simply means being unwilling or hesitant to do things that were not *our* idea or that were not done in the way *we* wanted to do them. This does not necessarily mean that we will not do the task. We will do it, but it is going to be with our jaw set. That is stubbornness. Working with a stubborn apprentice is a lot like trying to drive a car with the brakes on. We must be willing to lay down our own ideas of how things should be done and be willing to be trained.

Highmindedness

Highmindedness is any thought or attitude that is self-exalting. Check any motivation or any goal with this question: *Does it exalt self or Jesus?* Anything that we want to do to exalt Jesus is close to the will of God. There might be a time when Jesus postpones an idea, but if it is going to bring Jesus glory, it is not selfish motivation, so do not be ashamed of good ideas that He gives you.

Another form of highmindedness is an *"I-can-do-it-better"* mentality. In the earlier days of my ministry I would listen to a particular youth minister that I was under and think, "Boy, he's not a very interesting preacher. You know, I could do better than that." I *knew* I could preach. I *knew* I could do a better activity than that. I *knew* I could do a better outreach than that. I *knew* I could run a better Bible school than that. But I soon learned, that attitude will not flow with authority. I was crossing out any chance I had at promotion. If I shared those "I-can-do-it-better" thoughts with others, it became open rebellion. God dealt with me and I quickly learned to eliminate the "I-can-do-it-better" mentality that blocks promotion.

I learned from Psalm 75:6-7, *promotion comes from God.* I learned that if God wanted me in a position, *He* was able to put me there. The only reason I was not in that position was because I had not prepared myself. There is no place for highmindedness in ministry.

A habitual lifestyle of unrepented sin

Talent and ability are only going to carry you so far. They might get you to the top or they might get you to a place where it looks like you are being promoted, but only godly character is going to keep you in that place of ministry.

> "For if we would judge ourselves, we should not be judged."
>
> 1 Corinthians 11:31

There will come a reckoning day when it is going to be: Judge yourself or be judged. In the time that I have been in ministry, I have seen some people that were really called and who could minister, and maybe even have some manifestation of signs and wonders, but they had a habitual lifestyle of unrepented sin. Unrepented sin is involvement in immorality, greed, pride, any habitual sin that someone refuses to give up. These people had deluded themselves into thinking that this lifestyle was acceptable because God apparently was still blessing them and they still had the ability to preach or to sing. You can cast out devils and heal the sick and still not be spiritually mature. God did not put up with that for long and the unrepented sin blocked promotion. Always remember — good or bad — payday cometh!

Attitudes of resentment, bitterness, or unforgiveness

We have to work at keeping our hearts pure. Offenses will come; Jesus forewarned us of that. Circumstances will arise in which we will have the opportunity to be hurt, and we will have to pass them by and walk in the love of Jesus. We will have to *choose* to extend forgiveness and mercy just like we need forgiveness and mercy extended to us. We need to have a tough hide and a tender heart to guard our heart against resentment, bitterness, and unforgiveness. If we have not experienced that already, we will. We must always remember to sow mercy, because there will be a day when we ourselves will need mercy.

Lack of discipline

This is where most people will miss it. We have good intentions, but we are not disciplined. Good intentions are not enough. How is our devotional life? How is our

Attitudes That Block Promotion

work life? Those things are important. Can we control ourselves? Can we control anger, temper, and fear? Are our words under control? Are our emotions under control? Is our stress level under control? When we are under stress, we are out of control and out of the will and peace of God. Do we control our own thinking? Or, are we depending on others to think for us, to set the pace for us, to create our opinions? Do we find it easy to get others to cooperate? Do we control our disappointments? Are we disappointed if we do not receive recognition for a job that we have done or for an idea that we come up with? Do we control our space? Do we keep our house or apartment or room clean? How is the closet? You may be asking, "what difference does that make?" All those things are manifestations of who we are and reflect how we represent Jesus. Can you imagine if the American Secretary of State were to show up at some of the high-level government meetings in foreign countries dressed in a pair of old ripped-up jeans and a sweatshirt, or with mustard stains all over their shirt? We insist that our representatives dress properly when they are going to speak for the President. By the same token, we speak for God. We are His representatives.

We cannot assume that God will bless our mess. We must do our part. It is all about, sowing and reaping. We must sow seeds of faithfulness and diligence. Then He will have something to bless and multiply back to us.

Burnout

Burnout is a loss of zeal and passion. It is losing our first love. Why do we desire to go into the ministry? Why do we desire to serve God? It is because we really love Him. When we lose sight of that, when we are not ministering for the love of Jesus, ministry becomes a drudge, a work, a weight. The yoke becomes heavy. I judge myself in this area all the time, because I do not want to go through the motions and miss God. I would rather leave the ministry and have my relationship with God and my family intact than be what the world would call a "successful minister" but lose my first love. Loving Him has to be the primary thing in life.

Self-promotion

Where does promotion come from? Again, Psalm 75 tells us that it comes from God, not from man. If God wants to put us in a place of leadership, it should be received as the adding of responsibility, to serve in a greater capacity. Promotion itself should not be the thing we are seeking.

Although Paul said it was an honorable thing for a man to seek the office of a bishop or a deacon, he gave that admonition because, at that time, being named to such an office could cost a man his life. So it was honorable, but not a thing of personal glory. He had to balance that against the Scripture that says, *"Seekest thou great things for thyself? Seek them not"* (Jeremiah 45:5). We are not seeking something for ourselves; we are seeking something that can only come from God, and we qualify that in our relationship as a minister to Him.

An unteachable spirit

Not only will having an unteachable spirit block our promotion, but it will also prevent us from increasing our skill and knowledge that we need to fulfill our calling. We will stop growing any time we develop an "I-know-it-all-and-you-can't-tell-me-anything" mentality. We must become knowledgeable, and we must remain teachable. Whether you are a youth minister, a plumber, a painter, a beauty consultant, make it your aim to become the most knowledgeable person in the field.

Being teachable means being willing to learn. We do not leap into a responsible position or ministry; it comes as another step along the way as we move forward spiritually. It also means submitting when a man or woman of God receives direction from God, and then transmits those goals to us. It teaches us to like doing what we normally would not. If I asked your pastor, youth minister, Bible school director or teacher, your *spouse, parents or your children,* would they agree that you are a teachable spiritual leader? Do you have regular assigned duties in your church or Bible school? Can you be trusted to handle a job? Do you find it difficult to arrive on time?

I tell those that work with me that "*On time*, is *late* for leadership." If I say we are leaving to go somewhere at seven o'clock, we are *leaving* at seven. I do not want my staff to *arrive* at seven, I want them there *before* seven. Why? Because that is when we meet. That is when service goes on behind the scenes. That is our preparation time. Being teachable is listening to others, learning to develop your talents and disciplining yourself to serve effectively.

We all need to do a heart check from time to time. We must evaluate ourselves to make sure that we do not slip in any area. That is another reason why spiritual apprenticeship is so important. We need to have someone to whom we are accountable, someone who can help us, in love, stay on top of things in our lives so that we do not block our promotion.

TOO MUCH TOO SOON

> *"I therefore, the prisoner of the LORD, beseech you that ye walk worthy of the vocation wherewith ye are called."*
> Ephesians 4:1

The word "vocation" literally means an invitation or calling. Many have said yes to the invitation, but disqualify themselves because of bad habits, negative attitudes or an unwillingness to judge themselves. Others have disqualified themselves because of impatience. The fact that we are told to "walk" indicates to me that there is a pace involved. Along the way, we develop the character to handle more of God's blessings — at His pace. When we are able to receive more without being distracted by the increase, we will receive more. It is all in due season. Do not be tempted to run ahead of God.

> *"Let patience have her perfect work, that ye may be perfect and entire, wanting nothing."*
> James 1:4

Be patient and God will cause you to come to full maturity. He will see to it that you lack nothing.

Spiritual Apprenticeship

Paul had Timothy as his disciple. Jesus had the Twelve. Elijah had Elisha. Elisha had Gehazi. Some servants in the Bible, and some today, have failed in their apprenticeship. Elisha's servant Gehazi is an example. His motivation was greed, and he was willing to lie, cheat and do whatever he could to get what he wanted. Gehazi's heart was not right. He apparently served faithfully for a while, especially in his dealings with the Shunammite woman (2 Kings 4), but when Elisha refused Naaman's money and gifts of clothing, Gehazi fraudulently obtained them. As a result, he was smitten with leprosy and dismissed (2 Kings 5:21-27). He ran after "things." He wanted to take a shortcut to the blessings.

I have seen many young ministers fall into the trap of wanting too much too soon, not taking into account that some of the men they are serving have taken years to get where they are. Those men have invested and sacrificed, and they have a proven track record of faithfulness to God. The blessings they have received are often the result of a lifetime of faithfulness. All some young ministers see are the benefits, and they sometimes lack the patience to sow and believe God for their own harvest. Rather than taking the time to learn stewardship, they borrow and charge credit cards to the limit all in an attempt to look prosperous. That is foolish.

> *"A faithful man shall abound with blessings: but he that maketh haste to be rich shall not be innocent."*
> Proverbs 28:20

There are no shortcuts! The foundation to being blessed is faithfulness. Many young ministers are willing to peddle their influence by promoting "get-rich-quick" schemes or by selling their church mailing list, only to give the ministry a black eye when deals fall through. Take the time to do things the *right* way, in a godly manner. If you are faithful, God will see to it that you have more than you have right now. Do not be in a hurry. Pace yourself.

Avoid the debt trap. It has been the snare that ruined many a marriage and ministry. Believe God for what you need and for abundance. If you are already in debt, believe God to deliver you and determine never to return. God wants His people as free from encumbrances as possible. He wants you to be blessed so you can be a blessing. *Begin today where you are.* If you have not been tithing, repent and start today. Be faithful. Wayne Myers, missionary statesman, says, "You can't claim God's promises while violating God's principles." It is not enough to *look* prosperous; God wants you to *be* prosperous. When you practice the principle, the promise will not be long in coming.

> *"If therefore ye have not been faithful in the unrighteous mammon, who will commit to your trust the true riches?"*
>
> Luke 16:11

Finances are part of the proving ground for the granting of spiritual riches. God wants to see how a young man or woman handles his or her financial resources. If you handle money as God desires, you may be a candidate to receive and be steward over the anointing.

Proper stewardship makes tithing the cornerstone. Next, the giving of offerings as the Lord directs. Paying your bills on time, as agreed, and establishing a savings account are also part of your stewardship program. What you are willing to compromise to obtain, you lack the strength to retain.

REMINDER TO LEADERS

"And the things that thou hast heard of me among many witnesses, the same commit thou to faithful men, who shall be able to teach others also."

2 Timothy 2:2

Someone has said that you have no right to hear from God twice until you have obeyed Him once. In the New Living Translation, 2 Timothy 2:2 reads, *"Teach these great truths to trustworthy people who are able to pass them on to others."* Paul was writing under the inspiration of the Holy Ghost. He was keenly aware that the Lord expects those who have matured in the things of God to pass on what they've learned. Paul took that commission seriously. One person can only do so much, but when that person trains others, and the others train others, the results are limitless. Paul knew that it was important to God that laborers for the Gospel be multiplied and spread throughout the world.

I've mentioned several times in this book that an apprenticeship is a mutually beneficial relationship. When we begin at the place of servanthood and learn from those we serve, we will mature and inevitably be promoted. God requires leaders to train up their own Elishas and Timothys. We must ask God to give us people that we can teach and sow into. The Lord has bestowed upon us certain knowledge and skills — a certain expertise. Now he expects us to pass them on.

An association of professional photographers has a clause that states that in order to join their association, you must agree to teach other people about photography. The point is to carry on the craft — to hand it down from generation to generation. It means having a heart that says, "I'm not going to hoard this skill. It's too valuable to let it die when I do." God's desire is for us to share. Freely we have been given; we are to freely give. We are to use our giftings to bless others. Those who have a similar calling should be able to come to us for training, instruction, and advice. Earlier we talked about "Dance with the one that brung ya." Who likes to go to a dance alone? Bring someone with you!

No Place for Personal Empires

Apprenticeship is not about using people; it's about developing people. It is a matter of raising up someone in the things of God and life so that a godly heritage remains in the earth. When you come to a position of leadership, you become responsible for somebody else. And God will hold you accountable for how you handle your relationships. The idea is not to figure out how to get our own private little work force or how to raise up our own personal empire. We should be equipping the saints for the work of the ministry. 1 Corinthians 3:21 says, *"Therefore let no man glory in men..."* God will not share His glory with anyone. We must do as we have been instructed. We must adopt the same attitude that Jesus had when He said in John 9:4, *"I must work the works of him that sent me, while it is day: the night cometh, when no man can work."* That includes training up others in what we've learned.

Pass the Baton

"A good man leaveth an inheritance to his children's children..."

Proverbs 13:22

This Scripture applies not only to our natural family, but it applies to our spiritual family as well. We are to have sons and daughters in the faith. We are to have those that we can raise up as spiritual children to leave a godly inheritance — those to whom we can pass the baton of our ministry.

"...For unto whomsoever much is given, of him shall be much required: and to whom men have committed much, of him they will ask the more."

Luke 12:48

Can you imagine what would happen in a relay race if the second runner finished his leg of the race and refused

Spiritual Apprenticeship

to pass the baton to the next runner? *"No! That's MY baton! I'm not giving it to you! Get your own!"* Or, what if the runner got to the next person and held onto the baton, running along side the other person saying, *"I know you want this baton and I really should give it to you. I know we want to win this race, but I'm afraid you might drop it. I want to help you and make sure that nothing goes wrong."* That would be it for them! They would be disqualified and lose the race! Passing the spiritual baton does not mean that you are out of the race. It just means that you, as a member of the Body of Christ, fitly joined together with the rest of the body, are willing to run the race to win! Each member of the team is vitally important. And we must be team players. There is no "us" and "them" in the body of Christ.

Stewardship, Sowing and Reaping

"The earth is the LORD'S, and the fulness thereof; the world, and they that dwell therein."
Psalm 24:1

"For the earth is the LORD'S, and the fulness thereof."
1 Corinthians 10:26

"...all things were created by him, and for him."
Colossians 1:16

We must realize that everything belongs to God. It's all His, whether it be finances, material things, our abilities, or the anointing. God has full ownership of everything. We are merely stewards. It is our spiritual duty, as

Reminder To Leaders

stewards of the anointing of God, to pass along all that we can to other faithful stewards. There is a law called the *Law of Sowing and Reaping*. It applies to the natural realm, and it applies just as fully to the spiritual realm. It is the law of "what goes around, comes around." It is true, what you make happen for someone else's house, God will make happen for yours. If you want to climb, turn and help someone else get up the mountain. When we turn to help somebody else, it serves to advance us as well.

It's all about advancing the Kingdom of God anyway, not about our own personal advancement. Some people are so overprotective that if you try to ask them questions about the ministry you can't ever get a straight answer out of them. It's almost as if they are afraid that if they share what they know, they won't be needed anymore. Helping someone else doesn't threaten "job security." It serves to enhance and solidify our own lives. That is where Joshua may have missed it. Perhaps the reason the strength of leadership ended with him wasn't because no one was willing to serve him. Maybe he failed to take someone under his wing to show them the ropes. Maybe he wanted to keep the baton on his mantle at home and didn't want to part with it. He may have neglected to plant what Moses taught him into someone else.

"So then neither is he that planteth any thing, neither he that watereth; but God that giveth the increase. Now he

that planteth and he that watereth are one: and every man shall receive his own reward according to his own labour. For we are labourers together with God: ye are God's husbandry, ye are God's building."

1 Corinthians 3:7-9

Let me encourage you. Help someone else. You only increase in what you invest. Investments take time, but a godly investment reaps big dividends. No farmer ever reaped a harvest on seed that he intended to sow. He must plant some seed. The more seed he plants, the bigger the harvest. Sow into someone else. There's a reciprocal thing that takes place. It's a win/win situation. If I help you do what's in your heart to do, we will both be winners. Help someone else fulfill their calling. When you help them succeed, you succeed. God honors a cheerful giver! With the call of God it is a matter of stewardship, rather than ownership. Let's take serious action on what Paul said to Timothy in 2 Timothy 2:2, *"...the same commit thou to faithful men, who shall be able to teach others also."* As we train up others in the things of God through apprenticeship, then we will hear Him say, *"Well done, good and faithful servant; thou hast been faithful over a few things, I will make thee ruler over many things: enter thou into the joy of thy Lord."*

CONCLUSION

I believe that it is your heart's cry to be all that God wants you to be, just like when I was crying out to Him that cold day in March. Otherwise, you wouldn't have picked up this book. God hears the heart cry of His children. As you prayerfully put the things you've read in this book into practice, you will be well on your way to achieving that goal. You will be positioning yourself for promotion. Let me encourage you, don't quit. You can get there from here and you will, as long as you do it His way.

I close in prayer:

Father, I thank You today that You are the Master, the head of the church. I thank You that You are able, because of Your infinite nature, to show favor to every one of us. You are able and willing to take us into relationships that are going to springboard us ahead from glory to glory, from one level to another.

Father God, I declare by faith today that the doors of promotion are much closer than many have thought. I declare that their faithfulness and service are going to increase, that they are going to serve You when they are serving others. I declare, in the name of Jesus, that You have Your hand upon these readers, and that the godly desire they have in their hearts will indeed come to pass. Thank You that You will send mighty men and women of God to teach and to train and to bring that spirit of excellence.

So, Father, I pray that the enemy will not be able to sidetrack anyone. I pray encouragement over them. I pray that the spirit of the conqueror in them today will know that promotion is coming as they become usable in the things of God. Father, I loose my faith in agreement with them that they are patiently, expectantly waiting by serving You and others with respect and honor.

Also, Lord, I thank You that leaders who read this book will have a new desire birthed in them to pour into the lives of key apprentice relationships. Give them wisdom and discernment. You set up the divine connections and appointments needed to match the correct leaders to the correct apprentices. As Paul committed to Timothy, may these leaders commit all they've learned, with love and care, into the lives of faithful stewards to continue Your legacy in the earth until the return of Jesus. We thank You for it. In Jesus' name, amen.

SALVATION PRAYER

- God loves us and has a wonderful plan for our lives. We can only achieve true peace and our full potential when we have a personal relationship with Him. It's sad, but most people don't achieve that peace and potential. Why?
- Because sin separates all mankind from God. The Bible says, *"All have sinned and come short of the glory of God"* (Romans 3:23). Active rebellion or passive indifference are signs of sin.
- He made provision for us through His Son Jesus. People try many different things to get to God, but Jesus is the only way we can be reunited in relationship with God. *"For there is one God, and one mediator between God and men, the man Christ Jesus"* (1 Timothy 2:5).
- God created us with a free will. We must choose to come to Him and invite Him into our lives. *"Yet to all who received Him, to those who believed in His name, He gave the right to become children of God"* (John 1:12).

If you would like that peace and union with God, simply speak to Him and mean it from your heart. Admit your need (I am a sinner). Be willing to turn away from your sins (repent). Believe that Jesus died for you on the cross and rose from the grave. Invite Jesus Christ to come in and direct your life through the Holy Spirit. (Receive Him as Lord and Savior.) You can use your own words, but here is and example:

> *Dear Lord, I am sorry for all of my sins and I want to turn away from them today, with Your help. Thank You for dying on the cross for me. I believe You rose from the dead, and are returning again – all for me. Come into my heart. Wash me, cleanse me, change me and set me free, fill me with Your Spirit and give me a hunger and passion for the things that You desire. Help me to live the full life You have for me. In Jesus' name I pray. Amen."*

If you prayed this from your heart and meant it, you have assurance form His Word, the Bible, that you are now a born-again, child of God and will spend eternity with Him. *"For whosoever shall call upon the name of the Lord shall be saved"* (Romans 10:13).

There are some important things you can do to grow in your relationship with Him. Read your Bible every day to get to know Him better. Invest time in prayer every day. Prayer is talking to God and listening to Him speak to your heart. Tell others about Him. Worship, fellowship, and serve with other Christians in a church that preaches Jesus Christ. Demonstrate your new life by love, concern and compassion for others. Welcome to the family!

If you prayed to receive Jesus Christ for the first time, please let us know. You can contact us at Calvary Cathedral International, 1701 Oakhurst Scenic Dr., Fort Worth, TX 76111. Or call us at 817.332.1246. We'd love to hear from you!

Author and minister, **Mark Carrillo**, is an associate minister at Calvary Cathedral International, located in Fort Worth, Texas. Mark is involved in leading the "Hour of Power" prayer revival services, as well as teaching in Calvary Cathedral International Bible School.

Mark and his wife, Lisa, have two children and live in Fort Worth, Texas.

FOR ADDITIONAL COPIES OF
SPIRITUAL APPRENTICESHIP

Please fill out the form below and mail with checks payable (**in U.S. dollars**) to:

Calvary Cathedral International
Attn: The Bookstore at Calvary
1701 Oakhurst Scenic Dr.
Fort Worth, TX 76111

U.S. SHIPPING	
$ 0.00 - $ 25	$ 3
$ 25.01 - $ 50	$ 4
$ 50.01 - $100	$ 5
$100.01 - $200	$ 7
$200.01 +	$10

The books are only $10.00 each
(plus shipping).

For more information, or for volume discounts, please call:
817.332.3736, or FAX your orders to
817.338.0300

Name: _____

Organization: _____

Address: _____

City, State, ZIP: _____

Quantity: _____ Payment Enclosed _____